Keeping the options open

The importance of maintaining a broad and flexible curriculum offer for adults

A DISCUSSION PAPER

Veronica McGivney

promoting adult learning

Published by the National Institute of
Adult Continuing Education (England and Wales)

Renaissance House
20 Princess Road West
Leicester LE1 6TP
Company registration no. 2603322
Charity registration no. 1002775

First published 2005

promoting adult learning

NIACE has a broad remit to promote lifelong learning
opportunities for adults. NIACE works to develop
increased participation in education and training,
particularly for those who do not have easy access
because of barriers of class, gender, age, race, language
and culture, learning difficulties and disabilities, or insufficient
financial resources.

For details of all NIACE's publications, please visit www.niace.org.uk/publications

Cataloguing in Publication Data
A CIP record of this title is available from the British Library.

ISBN 1 86201 243 1

Cover design by Prestige Filmsetters
Designed and typeset by Boldface, London EC1
Printed in Great Britain by Latimer Trend & Company Ltd, Plymouth

Keeping the options open

The importance of maintaining a broad and flexible curriculum offer for adults

A DISCUSSION PAPER

Contents

Acknowledgements

This paper is based on a review of existing research evidence and verbal and written communications from education providers, practitioners, researchers, and analysts.

I would like to thank all the following for sending comments, information and written materials and, in some cases, for giving up time to discuss issues arising in their work: Nicola Aylward, Jan Eldred, Julie Gabriel, Kate Goad, Jeanne Haggart, Silvanna Harvey, Yola Jacobsen, Peter Lavender, Liz Maudslay, Bethia McNeil, Bryan Merton, Rachel Spacey, Chris Taylor.

I would also like to thank the practitioners working with people with literacy, language and numeracy needs, adults with learning difficulties, and other groups who supplied comments and information. As a number of these did not wish their name or organisation to be identified, it is considered best, for the sake of confidentiality, that all should remain anonymous.

I am particularly grateful to Andy Kail for his help with finding relevant literature and to Peter Lavender for his helpful comments on the text.

Veronica McGivney

Preface

Traditionally local authorities, further education colleges and (some) voluntary organisations have provided a wide range of learning programmes for adults. In his letter of remit for the newly established Learning and Skills Council, the former Secretary of State for Education and Employment, David Blunkett, referred to this as the 'great heritage of adult and community education which developed in the 19th century, on which the council should build 'to restore a commitment to learning' (Blunkett, 2000).

While there are considerable geographical disparities in provision, adult learning opportunities overall in England are rich and varied. There is growing concern, however, about the narrowing or closure of programmes in some locations, institutions and curriculum areas in response to policy pressures and funding constraints. Whether the current volume and diversity of learning opportunities will survive will depend on the momentum towards meeting national skills targets and the impact of new proposals for the planning and funding of adult provision.

This paper discusses the threat and its implications. It explores the assumptions about 'usefulness' that underlie current priorities and suggests how government priorities can be, and are being, met through the maintenance of a broad and flexible curriculum offer. It argues the need to maintain a range of learning provision that is affordable and accessible to adults and responds to their diverse interests and needs.

While we agree with Tomlinson (FEFC, 1996) that the content of learning cannot be separated from how it is organised, taught and delivered, the primary focus of the paper is restricted to the maintenance of a varied and balanced programme offer for adults.

What is happening to the curriculum for adults?

In their policy discussion paper on areas of consensus and debate in the recognition and recording of achievement in non-certificated learning, Turner with Tuckett (2003, pp. 1–2) describe the adult curriculum as:

a rich mix that includes: liberal arts, crafts and the performing arts; learning for active citizenship, community activism and regeneration; return to learn and return to work courses; personal development programmes; provision for adults with learning difficulties and disabilities; liberal studies such as local and natural history, current affairs and environmental sciences; courses that are internally certificated, possibly linked to accredited programmes; and ICT-based learning.

Is this rich mix now under threat?

The government's *Skills for Life* (*SfL*) strategy and Level 2 entitlement are positive and valuable moves to focus on the least qualified and to raise qualification and skill levels in the population. For this they have been warmly welcomed. However, they may be having unintended consequences. There are growing concerns that pressures on providers to meet national priorities and targets are leading to a significant narrowing of the curriculum for adults. As has happened in the past, learning that is deemed to lead to approved national qualifications and increase 'employability' is given priority over other forms of learning that are assumed to be pursued for their own sake or for self-development, recreational or other reasons. Such a distinction is usually made purely on the strength of the title and content of programmes without reference to learners' purposes for learning or the outcomes of their learning.

Government priorities relating to the post-16 sector are unequivocal and are expected to be addressed by the Learning and Skills Council (LSC):

We will focus our money and efforts on young people, adults without five GCSE equivalents and those currently out of work. This means our priorities are 16–18-year-olds, apprentices, anyone without literacy, language and numeracy and anyone without a full level 2 qualification. (Jon Gamble, LSC director of adult learning, quoted in Kingston, 2005)

1

Given the limitations of these priorities, there was widespread relief when the Skills Strategy (DfES, 2003) promised to safeguard in each LSC area, a range of learning opportunities for adults, including learning for culture, leisure, community and personal fulfilment:

> There must continue to be a broad range of opportunities for those who get pleasure and personal fulfilment from learning. A civilised society should provide opportunities to enable everyone, including those who have retired, to learn for its own sake. (DfES, 2003, para 4.40)

The intention, as elaborated in the LSC consultation document on taking forward the Skills Strategy (LSC, 2004a), is to address unevenness and disparities in the scale, funding and quality of non-accredited provision by supporting one type of adult learning, 'First Steps', through mainstream funding, and learning for personal and community development through a block grant. The latter will include family learning, learning for older people, learning for active citizenship and community development, learning through cultural activities, and work with libraries, museums and art galleries. A national budget for these kinds of learning will be distributed to local LSCs (LLSCs), with allocations weighted according to the socio-economic profile of each area.

It is likely, however, that the overall funding available for such provision will be small, and providers will be expected to make up the shortfall from higher fees.

> We want a system that both ensures that all adults have access to a wide range of learning opportunities and encourages well qualified adults and adults learning for their own pleasure and recreation to make an appropriate contribution to costs. (LSC, 2004a, para. 4.2)

The LSC assumes that fees will rise from 25 per cent to 27.5 per cent of basic course costs in 2005–06. Young people, those studying literacy, language and numeracy (LLN) or aiming for a first Level 2 qualification, and people on income-based benefits will receive free tuition, and fee concessions will be available to older learners on income-based benefits or who receive the pension credit. Decisions about funding arrangements for 2006–07 have yet to be made.

Death by a thousand cuts?

Despite these commitments, a number of providers have doubts about their ability to maintain the same volume and diversity of programmes for adults. There have already been programme cuts and closures in some local education authorities (LEAs), in response to pressures from LLSCs to concentrate specifically on the government's key priorities. According to some adult education organisers, certain local authorities have set limits on the types of programmes they are prepared to support: 'Our LEA won't fund anything now unless it's vocational'.

There have also been an increasing number of reports that further education (FE) colleges (the main providers of programmes for adults in some areas) are dropping some or all of their courses and programmes that, for funding purposes, fall into the category of 'other' provision (non-certificated work that does not make an immediate contribution to national targets).[1]

'Other provision' is a significant element in the overall programme offer of many colleges and its actual or threatened erosion is causing considerable alarm among those working with or on behalf of adult learners, as demonstrated by the following comments:

> *More than 10 per cent of general FE colleges did more 'other' work last year than all the rest of their activity combined [...] 'Other' means 'not in the National Qualifications Framework'. The concept of such a framework was seductively attractive when first proposed, but in practice it has been and continues to be misleading and dangerous.* (Flint, 2005, p. 25)
>
> — — —
>
> *Other provision is a pot of money unconnected with government priorities and it's getting smaller and smaller'.* (College worker with people with learning difficulties)
>
> — — —
>
> *Narrowing the adult curriculum is leading us into disaster. I'm still passionate about the 'comprehensive curriculum' for adults but my prediction of a return to the Victorian model is becoming all too real. (FE manager)*
>
> — — —
>
> *The AOC says it has been fielding calls since last autumn from colleges reporting warnings from LLSCs about caps on funding for adult courses* (Kingston, 2004a)
>
> — — —
>
> *[some] colleges and/or their local learning and skills councils (LSCs) are saying that there is no cash for courses falling outside the government's priorities – the 16–19 age group and adults lacking literacy, language and numeracy.* (Kingston, 2004b)
>
> — — —
>
> *Funding linked specifically to targets is causing problems in the FE sector. There are some reports that further funds have not been made available for 19+ education and training that is unrelated to government targets, which focus on literacy, language and numeracy.* (LSRC, 2004, p. 28)

Anxieties about the implications for adult learning of course closures and higher fees have also prompted questions in the House of Commons (Kent, 2004).

---

1 The Learning and Skills Act of 2000 listed the learning provision that would be recognised and supported by the LSC under two headings – 'qualifications' (programmes leading to approved qualifications) and 'other' (all other provision). 'Other' provision includes the whole range of non-accredited programmes: the liberal arts, crafts and the performing arts; personal development programmes; community-based programmes; return to learn and access courses, and provision for students with learning difficulties and disabilities, as well as programmes leading to internal awards and certificates.

It seems, however, as Tuckett (2004) suggests, that some LLSCs have misinterpreted the government's intention and have reacted prematurely, advising the organisations and institutions they fund to concentrate mainly on programmes that meet the national priorities. As a result, some LEAs and colleges have started to cut non-certificated adult programmes, fearing that LSC funding for those that do not contribute to specific targets will be curtailed (Kingston, 2004b).

Learning to improve literacy, language and numeracy

Skills for Life (*SfL*) is one of the government's greatest educational priorities and there has been a huge investment in it. It has already generated impressive results. There has been a significant increase in the numbers of learners and organisations involved, a sharpening of curriculum focus and significant production of relevant curriculum materials. According to practitioners, the improvement of skills has enhanced the lives of many people. Nevertheless, pressure to meet the LLN targets[2] is one of the most frequently cited reasons for the reduction or distortion of the adult curriculum. As Lavender (2004) points out, there has been a shift from Moser's (1999) original focus on improving functional LLN to a focus on improving the numbers of people with qualifications up to and including Level 2 (DfEE, 2000a). LLSCs have been advised to give funding priority to courses in adult basic skills that lead to qualifications. All of the LLSC offices have a target to meet, set by the LSC as a proportion of the *SfL* national targets. Provision based on the national standards but which does not lead to an approved, national qualification is defined as 'other provision,' the main purpose of which should be to encourage those not yet ready for a qualification or to widen participation. Each LLSC can decide how much of this they are willing to fund. Some, however, are threatening to fund only provision in which learners take the test. This is encouraging some providers to get learners through the qualification or to just 'teach the test'. Some have also extended LLN learning and assessment to people who neither need nor want them.

Evidence of this comes from a number of sources. A sample of comments received from LSC-funded institutions and organisations suggests that some regret what they see as the replacement of a learner-centred approach with one that is driven by external targets:

> *The guidance on funding and embedded learning means that we have stopped offering embedded provision on our ACL programme – it's discrete literacy, language and numeracy provision or nothing. There has been some pressure on tutors/organisers to persuade learners to take the test, but in the three groups I set up over the last year with 30 learners (all of whom were anxious first-time adult learners) none wanted to.*

---

2 In 2001, the government committed to helping 750,000 adults obtain LLN qualifications in England. This commitment has been extended to improve the literacy and numeracy skills of 2.25 million adults by 2010, with an interim target of 1.5 million by 2007.

The first question they asked at the information and advice session was 'do I have to take an exam?' There was definite resistance to the idea, even when expressed as an entitlement. (SfL worker, WEA)

— – —

I feel some concern with some of the current thinking which pushes accrediting current skills in preference to assessing need followed by teaching and learning to increase knowledge and skills. My personal feeling is that this approach is SfL-target-driven rather than individual-need-driven. One of my roles is to offer initial interviews to prospective learners and all of those seen since September this year have the goal to improve their skills. None have come with the stated aim of gaining an accreditation! (LEA Curriculum Manager for Skills for Life)

Another LLN specialist disputes some of these comments, arguing that assessing needs is still very important in LLN and that discussion about tests should only take place when learners are sufficiently confident to undertake them. There is little doubt, however, that some providers are being strongly encouraged to offer the tests to as wide a group of learners as possible:

We are sure from all our feedback that colleagues feel under great pressure to offer courses which lead to the test and which can distort the purposes for which learners present for wanting to learn (e.g. if you want to develop writing you end up being asked to do a reading test as the test is only for reading, at the moment). Some folk seem able to handle this by weaving what learners want around the assessment for the test but others find that very difficult. (LLN co-ordinator, national organisation)

— – —

There are complaints from some lobbies (for example, those dealing with disability) that teachers and providers are making everyone do literacy, language and numeracy and tests etc that they don't need. Even the literacy, language and numeracy lobby itself is telling us that there's more to life than literacy and numeracy. (Director, voluntary organisation)

A voluntary centre that offers a range of education and training courses, including LLN, for women, and which has an excellent record of widening participation in learning, is struggling to maintain its other provision in the face of LSC pressure to concentrate more on contributing to the *SfL* targets:

We've been under pressure for the last three years related to the types of courses we run and the level we run them at. We're very good at widening participation , but what we do doesn't meet local targets for ABE and ESOL so we're unpopular with the LLSC.

As a service we have always enrolled all learners on non-accredited courses and changed them to an accredited qualification aim when they are ready. Then we give them encouragement to take an appropriate accreditation. (Worker in voluntary organisation)

The centre has found that other provision acts as a convenient starting point for users who then often move into LLN and IT courses and from there, frequently, into employment.

> *Since 2000 we've trying to bring creative courses back and we now offer a programme 'Improving Personal Resources' – Tai Chi, self-defence, woodwork, assertiveness, improving confidence, job search. All counts as 'other provision'. People doing these often move on into our other courses. We suggest how they could do other things such as English and maths, IT. Many then go into other courses and then into employment. A lot of our learners go from there into work.*

Although Open College Network accreditation is used in some courses at the centre, workers have found that any mention of assessment is a turn-off for potential learners:

> *We don't want to be driven by qualifications and make this our main role. We look at each student as an individual. They come often with the expectation that they're not going to achieve and if you mention tests and assessment, they'll run away before they start. Once you've got them in the door they can start to look at other things. If you put them off at the start because they don't want qualifications, you may have lost them forever.* (Worker, voluntary organisation)

This is a familiar concern. A study in the UK and Sweden of learning programmes designed for new groups of learners indicated that:

> *placing the onus on qualifications and 'hard' outcomes could have a regressive or even detrimental effect on the progression of the learner. Learner confidence, once undermined, may be irretrievable.* (NIACE, 2003a, p. 38)

There is, however, evidence of a grapevine effect among providers. Some who have not themselves been asked to alter their curriculum have heard of pressure being applied by LLSCs in other areas:

> *Although I do not at present feel under pressure from my institution when coding up courses to personal targets for literacy, numeracy and ESOL, I know providers are coming under pressure from the local LSC to put as many adults as possible through the national tests in order to meet government targets. I understand that in some parts of the country people who do not really have problems with literacy and numeracy are being paid to take the tests in order to boost the figures.* (College Head of Literacy, Numeracy and ESOL)

Other institutions have already fundamentally altered their approach so that it is more geared towards meeting the *SfL* targets:

> *New provision here is only considered if it is geared towards targets. A whole new layer of courses has been developed and the explicit aim is to help the organisation*

achieve its targets. This is written into the curricular policy. There is no other consideration at all. Thus no Entry level classes have been discussed. Courses have been set up on a 10 week basis – to capture students who actually may already come to the college with level 1 skills – but who will be ready to take a test in 10 weeks.

The literacy learning of adults is of interest only in as much as it contributes to targets. A student who wants to develop broader skills in writing is explicitly written into the organisation's policy as 'not really suitable for Skills for Life targets'. The accusation is that they are taking a place away from someone who may want a qualification.

The college approach has been to set up embedded courses that incorporate testing and literacy, language and numeracy delivery as by-products of subject delivery. Some students have joined these classes because they are free and offer a gentle way into a college that traditionally only works with highly qualified skilled professional adults. The literacy test has been an intrusion which they have accepted because they have no choice but to. In a handful of instances students have dropped out when the test was explicitly mentioned. (Manager, *Skills for Life* Initiatives)

Neglect of those with lowest skill levels

This exemplifies one of the problems repeatedly mentioned by informants – the increasing difficulty, because of the *SfL* targets, to work with learners with the lowest level of skills who take longer to achieve. Some colleges that enrolled large numbers of people below Level 1 in 2004–05 are now being asked by the LSC to enrol learners at a higher level as this will result in a greater contribution to the targets.

A number of LLN managers report that they have experienced similar pressure to switch from carefully tailored programmes with new and often hard-to-reach groups, to higher level and accredited work with more advanced students:

We will need to access other funding streams to try and work with people who do not sit within the top end of Entry or level 1 or 2. (College Community and Workplace Development Co-ordinator)

– – –

In this county, there is real evidence of a change in the courses being provided. Up until recently, our learners were encouraged to work towards an OCN [Open College Network accreditation] as a first step, and then when they had more confidence to work towards a qualification. The OCN was specifically written for SfL Learners and is mapped to the curriculum. There are 43 units in it, and learners enjoyed putting together a portfolio which was based on the topics they wanted to learn. Certificates were often achieved after only one term's work.

Now we have been told by the LSC that we are offering too much 'other provision' and must look at our learners gaining accreditation that meets the national target. We haven't actually been told not to work with Pre-Entry or Entry Level 1 and 2 learners. However, we have been told that we should emphasise higher level provision in our publicity to actively encourage learners at top Entry Level 3 and Levels 1 and 2. (LLN Curriculum Manager)

We have had a lot of success in recruiting hard-to-reach learners who have very low literacy levels. Placement at too early a stage on courses leading to accreditation in response to a local LSC imperative to cut down 'other provision' has detrimental effects. Some learners are daunted by the prospect of accreditation, at least at first, and retention rates have declined. Because many learners take more than an academic year to take a qualification and because we encourage enrolment at all times of the year, some students are not achieving the qualification aim by the end of the year and being regarded by the LSC's mechanistic MIS as 'failed'. This means that our retention, achievement and success rates – as measured by the systems in place – have significantly declined in Skills for Life.

We have, however, greatly increased our contribution to the national 'literacy, language and numeracy' qualifications targets by persuading learners on all sorts of non-literacy, language and numeracy courses to take accreditation. Result – on paper we are moving forward in literacy, language and numeracy, but our ability to teach adults with very low literacy levels to read and write is impaired as this does not 'score'. (Principal Adult Education Officer, LEA)

– – –

In ESOL [English for speakers of other languages] *we have a huge number of learners with survival English needs. Colleagues are working hard to meet this demand but it will take years of intensive work for learners illiterate in their own language to 'achieve'. We also find that at E2* [Entry Level 2], *ESOL learners have enough English skills to find a job and support their family, and leave our provision – success or failure?* (Essential Skills Manager, LEA)

– – –

As a major provider of first step learning in literacy and ESOL, most of our learners are at the lower entry levels. We have a 25% increase in learners compared to this time last year – but they're the 'wrong' ones! It seems the Gremlins Campaign has had a good effect in motivating those with very poor literacy and numeracy needs to come forward, but this cohort is not yet ready to 'achieve' in government terms.

This is an issue that really concerns us. Our local LSC has committed extra funds for meeting SfL targets at E3 [Entry Level 3] *and above, but have re-iterated that our focus must change to go for 'low hanging fruit' (!) to meet our huge underachievement in government targets.* (Essential Skills Manager, LEA)

As a result of pressure to meet the targets, outreach work with particularly vulnerable groups is under threat in some areas:

I know from experience that institutions are focusing on targets and not on learners' needs. Just recently two colleges, have had their outreach provision withdrawn and this will impact on the relationships we had built up with them. (Lifelong Learning Co-ordinator, national voluntary organisation)

– – –

In our college we are currently undergoing a severe audit by management of all our Skills for Life provision and I gather that anything running with less than eight in a group will be closed. This means that where we have classes set up in community agency premises, such as community alcohol team Dry House or sheltered workshops where the students/clients have needs apart from Skills for Life, and there is not physically room to be teaching 8 at once, the provision will have to cease. Also in these venues the clients do not want to be working towards accreditation, they just need practical everyday skills to help them cope with life – reading numbers on a bus, reading instructions on food packets etc. Reading letters from benefits agency by themselves. Being able to turn up for interviews on time.

I think that this current funding regime will mean that we will not even be targeting clients in the various agencies who work with some of the socially excluded in the community. (College Community and Workplace Development Co-ordinator)

Some development officers working with young people have also expressed concerns about the impact of pressures to achieve targets both on the curriculum and on the motivation of learners:

Whilst providers are keen to develop provision with no (or no specified) accreditation, or not related to progression into employment, they are aware that they are unlikely to find or receive funding for this type of provision.

Providers hoping to work in partnership with local colleges are aware that practitioners working in the SfL arena are likely to want to stick more rigidly to the curriculum, which may not be appropriate for young adults.

On programmes such as E2E [Education to Employment], *where provision is more closely organised around a curriculum or framework, anecdotal evidence suggests learners simply move from one form of provision to the next as they are often unable/ unwilling/unprepared to 'achieve' within the boundaries of the curriculum framework.*

A lack of confidence around the curriculum (it is an unknown quantity for many working with young adults) discourages many practitioners from attempting to develop new provision. Private training providers are definitely less likely to try and develop provision working outside the curriculum and accreditation. Many practitioners feel constrained and pressurised to achieve unrealistic and inappropriate targets relating to the curriculum and accreditation, which ends up taking precedence over other issues (arguably more important when working with young adults) such as engagement and motivation. (Worker in national organisation)

Another practitioner acknowledges that while some programmes have been closing down, an accredited curriculum can be of great benefit in work with young adults. He suggests that the narrowing of the curriculum is largely due to other factors:

> *There is evidence that in some areas open-access provision is closing down but I would attribute low take-up as much to under-investment and poor programme offer as to the pressure to have learning and achievement accredited. I think there are many voices in the sector responding positively to the guidance and targets that have been set on recorded and accredited outcomes.*

However, the worries about the curriculum expressed by informants do not focus specifically on the merits or otherwise of accreditation per se. The comments from across the country cited above suggest that practitioners are more exercised by the issue of the appropriateness of accreditation for certain groups, and the timing of its introduction. A worker involved with young people with mental health difficulties believes that the imposition of accreditation and other targets is not always relevant for this group of learners. Learning to assist recovery is a more important concern:

> *Funding that is linked to regular uninterrupted attendance and accredited outcomes and targets is largely inappropriate for learners with mental health difficulties and can prevent them from accessing provision. Many practitioners have told us that developing confidence in this group of learners can be a long process. Some may wish to follow an accredited route when they feel more confident and secure, but others may never wish to do so.*

The situation varies, however, in different LSC areas. As one *SfL* co-ordinator pointed out, 'I think a lot has to do with the local LSC and how they see things'. Some LLSCs have been found more understanding than others about the time it takes for some learners to achieve the desired level of accreditation:

> *The targets are sometimes difficult to achieve because the focus is on the hard to reach client groups. We are always going to get people that will start a course and then for a variety reasons do no complete. The LSC understand it is sometimes impossible to reach all the targets, with our client groups. It is important that the LSC programme manager is updated periodically so they are aware of any difficulties.*

> *I have never been influenced or discouraged when working with people I know will not achieve accreditation or progression. These are the very people, I need to be working with.* (SfL worker, training organisation)

Other LLSCs appear to have reacted prematurely to what they see as a policy imperative, and are interpreting the targets very narrowly:

> *We know that LLSCs are the gate-keepers in this as we are repeatedly told by ABSSU [Adult Basic Skills Strategy Unit] that learners do not have to take the*

test and their own learning goals are fully fundable. In reality, because there is pressure to meet the targets, such provision is being discouraged by the LLSCs so that they can meet their targets. We also know that providers have to be very careful about putting on provision for older people where qualifications are far less important for the learners and where outcomes do not necessarily lead to progression to vocational learning/employment routes. (LLN co-ordinator, national organisation)

Despite pressures to meet *SfL* targets, some practitioners have managed to maintain a wide curriculum through developing an embedded LLN approach. One has found that meeting the targets this way has had benefits:

When the Skills for Life agenda took off and the government began to throw all the money at it, there was a real feeling that 'other provision' would suffer. As a manager I had to rethink and in the end we put the whole of the supported learning provision under the Skills for Life banner. We embedded literacy, language and numeracy into all we did, cross-referencing targets to the PECF [pre-entry curriculum framework] when we could. It was not all bad and in fact at times was very helpful. The added benefit, of course, was the fact that I could draw down additional support funds to support the learners. However, if I found a great art tutor, for example, she/he would have to be trained in using the PECF and this was discouraging to tutors. (Lifelong Learning Co-ordinator, national voluntary organisation)

Moreover, not everyone thinks the focus should be on those with the lowest skill levels. In their evaluation of new and flexible models of Move On and Get On at Work,[3] Dimmock and Foster (2004) comment on the effectiveness of an approach that switches from the 'labelling of need' to the offer of qualifications, specifically the National Certificates in Adult Literacy and Numeracy at Levels 1 and 2. Instead of focusing only on traditional Entry Level learners, the new models are aimed at those from Entry Level 3 to almost 'test-ready' for Level 2 who might benefit from raising their literacy and numeracy skills: 'The evaluations indicated that the models were reaching many previously unreached people from the 'upper' sector of literacy, language and numeracy needs (at Levels 1 and 2)' (Dimmock and Foster, 2004, p. 77).

While the evaluation suggests that these programmes are successfully meeting one area of learner need, there is a persisting question about help for those at the lower skill levels. It is paradoxical that a national programme, *SfL*, which is designed to improve adult LLN, is leading in some areas and institutions to the neglect of people with the poorest skill – those one would assume to be in need of greatest assistance from education services. This situation has come about largely in response to the clear funding priorities set out in the White Papers on skills:

---

3 The *Move On* national project is a component in the *SfL* initiative.

Wherever possible, we want adults to aim for basic skills at the Level 2 standard. We will encourage that through the Learning and Skills Council's (LSC) business cycle. We will increasingly prioritise within the allocation of LSC funds Skills for Life programmes leading to Level 2, and focus available LSC funds on those basic skills programmes that incorporate the Skills for Life standards, guaranteeing worthwhile progress and measurable achievement for learners. (DfES, 2005, p. 116)

People below Entry Level 3 are not a priority unless they are working towards that level. This effectively leaves out many people with very low basic skills or learning difficulties.

Loss of curriculum development and innovation

Pursuit of the targets seems also to have discouraged curriculum development and innovation. National research (NIACE, 2003a) encountered considerable frustration among LLN managers about the constraints on creative curriculum development resulting from attempts to meet the targets, and this was echoed in verbal reports and correspondence from practitioners:

I could foresee a scenario where the LSC ceases to fund courses which lead to personal targets and I think this would have a major effect on innovative development work. (College Head of Literacy, Numeracy and ESOL)

The testimony from practitioners about the narrowing of the LLN curriculum prompts the question: What is basic education actually for? Gilbert (2004) answers as follows:

It is to enable those who don't have it to become literate, numerate and to cope in an increasingly complex society so that they can maintain and advance themselves and their families. In other words, it is not an end in itself, and, by definition, does not necessarily or essentially lead to a demand for qualifications. (Gilbert, 2004, p. 20)

While such a definition does not rule out the use of accreditation to recognise achievement, it acts as a useful corrective to the single-minded pursuit of accreditation at all costs that is evident in some current practice.

Work with people with learning difficulties and/or disabilities

Practitioners working with adults with learning difficulties and/or disabilities have expressed identical concerns about the narrowing of programmes for this group of learners. Their comments also indicate that fears about possible withdrawal of funding are not only distorting the curriculum offer but discouraging providers from accepting the full range of learners.

Although much of the work with adults with learning difficulties and/or disabilities has traditionally been non-accredited, there are signs that there has been a major shift in recent years to offering a curriculum that will make a greater contribution to LLN targets:

> *Loads of people have approached me at training events etc. saying that they have had their funding or programmes cut. I've had comments like 'I can't fund my art class unless I call it basic skills', and, 'we used to have wonderful provision for people with complex needs but it's no longer funded because it's not accredited'.*

> *People are putting work with people with learning difficulties under literacy, language and numeracy in order to get funding. There are some places where they are using the Pre-Entry framework for literacy, language and numeracy for people with learning difficulties, but it hasn't worked because the learners weren't reaching the targets. But the targets are unrealistic for this group.* (Development officer, voluntary organisation)

— – —

> *The huge dominance of the literacy agenda is skewing provision. It's easier to draw down funding for literacy, language and numeracy. The issue is one for senior management: what learning they will agree to fund. Practitioners have come up with wonderful curricula for their learners but are told that they couldn't do it because they wouldn't get funding for it. There is misguided use of curriculum with people who have no voice. It's a long way from what 'Inclusive Learning' was about, which was about changing the curriculum agenda. We're still struggling to catch up with what is wrong with the curriculum. The Inspectorate has found that the curriculum for people with learning needs is the weakest area of all.*

> *It's a minefield we're working in. It's being done to disabled people rather than empowering them. A lot of learners have very little choice when they want to return to learn. They don't have access to the breadth of learning opportunities. There are huge assumptions made about what people need and want to learn.* (Practitioner working with people with learning difficulties and/or disabilities)

— – —

> *We have been receiving expressions of concern from staff working with learners with learning difficulties. We have had reports of managers or LLSC staff making comments such as 'you need to change your learning difficulty provision into a literacy, language and numeracy course'. All of this is particularly depressing in a context where the Department of Health in 'Valuing People' is actively advocating the importance of person-centred planning where service providers respond to individual wishes and aspirations rather than individuals fitting into prescribed systems.* (Worker in national organisation for people with disabilities)

Some practitioners feel that what is happening with the curriculum offered to this group of learners departs radically from the learner-centred approach advocated in the influential Tomlinson report for the Further Education Funding Council (FEFC, 1996):

Although a policy document (FEFC, 1996) emphasised the need for colleges to respond to individual learner requirements and address individual learning styles, there was a huge expansion in the number of national awards for students with learning difficulties. However, concern was expressed that the pressure to follow externally validated awards was leading some practitioners to use the award as a substitute for planning curricula based on individual priorities.

In such cases curriculum design becomes teacher-led and based on what the learner cannot do, rather than looking at learner potential, learner aspiration and the interaction of the learner with their environment. (Maudslay and Nightingale, 2004, p. 15)

According to Maudslay and Nightingale (2004), the Qualifications and Curriculum Authority (QCA) guidance on designing a learner-centred curriculum for young people with learning difficulties (2002) includes a number of case studies which demonstrate how the needs of a range of learners with learning difficulties can be met through very varied programmes. Conversely, they cite research which has found that many of those attending discrete programmes in colleges are not clear how the programmes meet their learning goals or connect with their aspirations.

Some providers have resisted organising discrete provision for learners with learning difficulties, offering them instead opportunities to participate in the whole range of curriculum areas offered to adults. In one LEA, for example, they can enter re-entry provision in all curriculum areas, although workers are braced for imminent change:

We've never gone down the SfL road with people with learning difficulties. We don't have a discrete programme area for LLDs, we have pre-entry areas across the curriculum and liaise with programme curriculum managers on what is needed. So they have access to all curriculum areas and traditional areas such as Healthy Living and Visual Arts. I don't assume that because people have a learning difficulty that they want to do SfL. They want to do music or painting or cookery or pottery. There's much greater demand for these than for SfL. Our curriculum has been consumer-led. We offer what people ask for.

We know that changes are coming and that there will be a tendency to put all our provision either into SfL or independent living. We don't like the divisions that the curriculum is about to be divided into. It's a major worry and a major step backwards. (Curriculum manager with responsibility for learners with learning difficulties)

As with LLN provision, the narrowing of the curriculum has sometimes come about in response to a perceived rather than imposed need, with managers conforming to what they see as the prevailing culture or the way things are going:

In the years immediately following the establishment of the Learning and Skills Council in 2000, the dominant pressure felt by teachers of adults with learning difficulties appears to be the perceived need to be following a 'literacy, language and numer-

acy' curriculum. Several teachers feel they have been pressurised into this curriculum area by their managers and this can result in learners following an inappropriate and narrow curriculum based on a limited and outcome-based notion of literacy, language and numeracy [...] Interestingly, this choice of curriculum came about through perceived rather than actual direction from above. [...] the LSC does not insist on these learners adhering to a literacy, language and numeracy programme. However [...] the prevailing culture, which was heavily biased in a particular direction, translated itself into practice. (Maudslay and Nightingale, 2004, p. 15)

Maudslay and Nightingale (2004) cite the DfES (2002) document *Adult Pre-Entry Curriculum Framework for Literacy and Numeracy* which shows how the framework does not need to be narrowly interpreted but can be used creatively to address individuals' needs.

There are widespread concerns about changes to some programme areas that appeal to people with learning difficulties and/or disabilities. One that is particularly popular with young adults is Education to Employment (E2E), which, according to practitioners, has been relatively creative in scope and has not previously required participants to take qualifications.[4] The funding for the programme was capped in 2004 and there are reports that accreditation will become mandatory and that specified accredited outcomes will be required within specified time limits. This will inevitably have the effect of excluding learners whose chances of achieving such outcomes are low:

Several people have expressed fears to us that the new E2E Guidance will exclude learners with learning difficulties and I have heard that one organisation (that traditionally worked very much with those with learning difficulties) are reorienting their provision to those who are likely to achieve level 2. (Worker with national organisation)

Maudslay and Nightingale (2004) cite an analysis of the new E2E guidance which shows:

how it guides contractors away from including young people who will not reach level 2. One LEA is particularly concerned as they have some very interesting small providers using E2E to support learners with learning difficulties and autistic spectrum disorder. (Maudslay and Nightingale, 2004, p. 36)

Such a shift away from the learners with lowest skill levels reflects what is happening in the LLN field.

---

4 E2E is targeted at young learners working below Level 2. Guidance on the programme (LSC, 2002, *Framework for Entry to Employment Programmes*) stressed the importance of creating flexible, individual programmes that met learners' needs and took account of views. External qualifications were not essential but could, where appropriate, form a part of the programme.

Family learning

The priority attached to LLN has had a strong impact on the curriculum of family learning. Family literacy, language and numeracy (FLLN) is linked to the *SfL* strategy. The aim of FLLN programmes is to improve the LLN skills of parents and to improve their ability to help their children's acquisition of LLN. A large new programme entitled *Skills for Families* – an ABSSU and LSC initiative working with LEA/LSC partnerships – is also mainly focused on LLN and capacity building for staff in LEAs.

Wider family learning (WFL) encompasses all family learning programmes which do not have acquisition of LLN as their primary focus, although some may contain elements of LLN. According to Horne (2004), such programmes:

> *include provision as diverse as family ICT, arts and crafts, family science, family football and parenting classes. It therefore includes some of the most fun and exciting family learning. Nevertheless, it can be seen, by some, as the poor relation of FLLN.*
> (p. 20)

This is because there are separate funding streams for FLLN and WFL and some feel that there is an element of unfairness in the disparity between them:

> *Political priorities are manifest in the funding streams. The greatest proportion are for family literacy and numeracy. The amount for wider family learning has been derisory.* (Family learning practitioner)

Yet, as Horne (2004) has observed, not all adults who wish to participate in family learning have LLN needs. In fact a NIACE (2003b) evaluation of LSC-funded family programmes found that nearly 66 per cent of LEAs had a higher demand for WFL programmes than they were able to supply and there was a strong sense that the *SfL* agenda was monopolising provision:

> *Many practitioners were worried that the Skills for Life agenda would encroach on wider family learning or that the sector would be overshadowed by an already relatively strong FLLN sector. Evidence [...] showed that the curriculum within LEAs appeared to be weighted towards supporting children's learning in a few key areas such as literacy and ICT.* (Horne, 2004, p. 132)

Despite disparities in funding, there is some evidence that WFL plays a greater part than FLLN in widening participation in learning and encouraging sustained learning. The NIACE evaluation indicated that it attracts more learners from disadvantaged groups and men, than FLLN. Research undertaken in Lancashire (Horne and Haggart, 2004) also suggests that it is more likely than FLLN to result in progression to further learning.

Given the priority attached in policy to educational progression, such findings undermine assumptions that WFL is of lesser value than family learning that aims to improve LLN. Once again, it seems, the *SfL* targets are determining the shape of an area of provision, although not to everyone's satisfaction:

> *Some LEAs were finding it hard to offer FLLN because the curriculum was so narrow and that intensive FLLN courses were too difficult for hard-to-reach people. There have been grumbles about constraints and inflexibilities.* (Family learning development officer)

The NIACE evaluation (NIACE, 2003b) concluded that there was still considerable work to be done in developing a broad and varied family learning curriculum within LEAs. This has been confirmed by an adult learning inspector who comments that inspections have not found a broad-based family learning curriculum in LEAs (Lamb, 2004, p. 13). The 2004 Adult Learning Inspectorate (ALI) summary report also states that while the range of provision has increased and there is greater choice and flexibility for learners, family learning programmes generally remain relatively narrow in scope: 'This reflects the current national funding priorities' (ALI, 2004, p. 24).

As in other areas of the curriculum, however, there is some confusion about what can and cannot be done with central funding. Practitioner comments at a conference on WFL (NIACE, 2003c) showed that although FLLN and WFL were both funded from the adult and community learning (ACL) budget, providers were not clear about what flexibility there was between the budgets. A case mentioned was an LEA that was not able to spend all its FLLN funding but was unable to use it for a highly successful WFL course that was actually feeding into FLLN courses.

Prison education

Another area where there is evidence of curriculum shrinkage is prison education. In 1997 a core curriculum was introduced in prison education, with a focus on basic education (literacy and numeracy, ESOL, key work skills, life skills, social skills, and IT).

A key performance indicator (KPI) was subsequently introduced in 2000, with the aim of reducing the proportion of prisoners discharged who are still at or below Level 1 for LLN. Key performance targets (KPTs) have been set for each establishment, specifying the number of nationally recognised literacy and numeracy qualifications to be achieved at Level 2.

Research indicates that these developments have had a negative impact on the scope of the curriculum offer in prisons. According to a researcher currently investigating this area:

There appears to be increasing evidence to suggest that the focus on LLN and assessment is restricting the curriculum offer. Resources appear to be focused increasingly on 'quick win' provision – i.e. offenders who can achieve the National Test without a lot of input. The approach appears to be squeezing vocational and art subjects, and provision for offenders with pre entry and entry needs. There are lots of issues here about the impact on engagement, motivation.

Other research (Braggins, 2001) has encountered dissatisfaction among prison staff and prison education workers who have found:

the very narrowness of the core curriculum is self-defeating. Many regretted the omission of the creative arts. As one governor put it: 'The curriculum broadly ignores the positive contribution creative education – e.g. art, music, dance and drama – can have when dealing with very damaged individuals with low self-esteem [...] and a low opinion of formal education'.

An experienced education manager [...] stressed the impoverishment of the programme as a result, as he sees it, of the demands of the core curriculum. 'We have no other educational provision [...] than that required by the core curriculum. This is a major deterioration in the programme [...] Our curriculum is narrower now than at any time in the last thirty years'.

The point that offering literacy and numeracy 'straight' was not going to lure the prisoner, however much she or he may need these skills, was made many times over. [...] It was not only the disappearance of the arts that worried many. [...] [One] noted that: '[the curriculum] ignores the fact that a lot of prisoners had bad experiences at school and would only choose more practical subjects. We have lost most of our practical courses, which had literacy, language and numeracy built into them, because of the national curriculum'.

Another warned that 'Literacy and numeracy alone are insufficient to render a prisoner employable.' [...] The curriculum was seen as particularly limiting for those with a responsibility for prisoners serving long sentences. (p. 25)

Braggins (2001) identified the introduction of the KPI as an even greater contributor to the narrowing of learning programmes than the core curriculum. While some of the prison staff interviewed felt that the targets had some advantages, the major concern they identified was the skewing and narrowing of the curriculum that was taking place in order to meet them.

More recently, the All-Party Parliamentary Group for Further Education and Lifelong Learning (2004) have found that while a range of academic, general interest and arts-based courses is still on offer across the prison estate, it varies widely from prison to prison. The main findings of their investigation are virtually identical to those of Braggins' (2001) research. They also chime with reports from the broader field of adult education practice about the dominance of the *SfL* targets:

> *The curriculum is dominated by basic skills training, leaving significant numbers of more able and/or longer-term prisoners with no educational and training opportunities. While the Prison Service is justly proud of its success in delivering against its targets for literacy, language and numeracy, measures have been geared to numbers of qualifications achieved, rather than the achievements of individual prisoners. Prisoners have been retaking the same qualifications in different prisons. In some prisons, all prisoners have been expected to take Level 1 and 2 exams, no matter what their ability.* (All-Party Parliamentary Group for Further Education and Lifelong Learning, 2004, p. 3)

The All-Party report includes numerous comments from prison education staff about the impact of the KPTs on the curriculum. Typical of these are:

> *The whole thing is driven by literacy, language and numeracy.*
>
> — – —
>
> *We do see every new prisoner. But we have to meet the targets for level 1 and 2. So we put them all through levels 1 and 2.*
>
> — – —
>
> *Prisoners may be put through the same exams in each new prison they are sent to, to 'get the numbers' for the prison.*
>
> — – —
>
> *KPTs lead to a focus on numbers achieving qualifications, rather than on meeting the needs of individuals. The classic is putting graduates through level 2 to 'get your targets'.*
>
> — – —
>
> *An emphasis on basic skills may be to the detriment of the more able prisoners. There are no targets for GCSEs or NVQs achieved, and only limited recording of degrees achieved by prisoners.*
>
> — – —
>
> *For longer serving prisoners there must be a broader focus than just the basic skills.*

(All-Party Parliamentary Group for Further Education and Lifelong Learning, 2004, p. 10)

The All-Party investigation found that the most popular courses among prisoners were those that developed not basic but practical skills. It appeared, however, that some prison staff and education officers were not aware that they could mount more adventurous and flexible programmes by embedding LLN within other subjects:

> *One contractor stressed that: 'It is not the case that all you can do is basic skills. You can run anything you want within the core curriculum. But governors think everything must go to achieve the targets.'*

An education manager commented: 'Integrating key skills into most of our provision has safeguarded some subjects within the curriculum, particularly visual arts.' Another noted that 'It depends how you apply it [the core LLN curriculum]. *It can be embedded in a creative framework.'*

Braggins (2001) had also found that prison and education staff were not clear about what was possible and what was not, within the existing curriculum.

As in other areas of adult education, it is sometimes managers' views and perceptions rather than overt outside pressure that result in the narrowing of the curriculum. One prison that gave evidence to the All-Party Group stands out in providing a wide range of learning opportunities, including courses in sociology, film studies, yoga, art, drama, access to journalism, parentcraft, preparation for work, money management, group and team work (including a discussion group), and cultural awareness. Despite their effectiveness in engaging prisoners, some of these activities are seen by managers as having little practical value:

The discussion class 'picks up a lot of stroppy individuals who find the route back to the learning track'. However the Governor told us that this might not survive – or at least, in his view, it was something that should happen in the evenings and weekends – since it was 'not something that will get people jobs.' (All-Party Parliamentary Group for Further Education and Lifelong Learning, 2004, p. 12).

· · · · ·

The evidence presented above suggests that, in some post-16 sectors and curriculum areas, there has been a significant narrowing and shrinkage of the range of learning programmes available to adult learners, either as a consequence of overt pressure from LLSCs, or from a premature pursuit of government targets by providers:

Some local LSCs are already seeking to increase first steps and accredited provision and requesting other change to existing patterns of non-accredited provision before they have been able to think through the intention behind the safeguard, the implications of these proposals, and the composition and size of the funding resource they may have in future to purchase provision.

The virtual invisibility of learning for personal and community development in the LSC's strategic priorities is likely to exacerbate this trend and is not helpful to the future of such provision. (NIACE, 2004, p. 5)

Reports from practitioners also suggest that there has been a dwindling of opportunities for people at the lowest basic skill levels (i.e. at Pre- Entry and Entry Levels 1 and 2): those whom one would expect to be given greatest priority in policy.

The *SfL* targets appear to be exerting a particularly strong constraint on programme range and innovation. Yet, as a NIACE (2003a) report on embedding LLN points out, it is possible to use a wide and flexible curriculum for achieving these. Programme areas that have been successfully used by a variety of providers to embed LLN delivery include sport, vehicle maintenance, cooking on a budget, local history, photography, tourism, catering, work skills, adult rural skills, hairdressing, and living skills. The report warns, however, that learners' purposes for engaging in the host subject must be paramount.

There are signs that the breadth of adult learning opportunities may continue to diminish in the near future. The combination of LLN targets and the requirement to meet the Level 2 entitlement could lead education providers to redesign some of their courses and reduce the number of those that do not contribute to these priorities.

The proposals to separate adult education that does not have approved external accreditation into 'First Steps' to be covered by mainstream funding, and learning for personal and community development to be covered by a combination of public subsidy and fee income (LSC, 2004a), could, unintentionally, result in the further narrowing of the diversity of provision for adults.

What are the implications of current developments?

For overall adult provision?

Despite the government's commitment to protecting learning for personal and community development, some expect that the combination of narrowed priorities and tighter resources could eventually erode a significant proportion of traditional adult education:

> *Anyone looking closely at prospects for the field must expect fairly bumpy times ahead. It is not just the threat to adult and community learning budgets but, more particularly, the danger for what is now called 'other further education' – that rich mix of worthwhile learning that sits outside the narrowness of the national qualifications framework. It is work that includes ESOL provision at entry level and the whole of the Workers' Educational Association grant. It also includes the flagship provision of specialist colleges like the City Lit in London, and much of the Open College Network accredited provision. This is not work that we can afford to see at risk.* (Tuckett, 2005, p. 7)

David Sherlock, Chief Inspector of Adult Learning, suggests that the new funding proposals 'could herald the most radical shake-up the ACL sector has experienced in recent years' (Sherlock, 2005, p. 19).

A number of concerns have been expressed about the new funding proposals. One is the view that personal and community development provision are significantly different areas of education and should not come under the same budget. It has been pointed out that it will be easier to charge higher fees for the former than for the latter. This could lead to a diminution of valuable learning activities aimed at community cohesion and regeneration.

Another concern centres on the potential impact on some areas of the curriculum, such as family learning.

For family learning provision?

Family learning is mentioned in the proposals under *SfL* and First Steps. This suggests that WFL will only receive secure mainstream funding if it is for people without a Level

2 qualification and can be recognised as part of a progression route. This may reduce the volume of family learning offered to parents and children (whom the document takes no account of). WFL for people who already have a Level 2 qualification or above will have to come under the safeguard, although it is hard to see how high(er) fees could be demanded for it. There is also a question about the inclusion of family learning in provision described as 'personal development,' although it might be more relevant to community development.

Family learning practitioners believe that the requirements of the First Steps definition will not sit well with the grain of current policies for children and families. Family Learning has a unique position in its provision for both parents (adults) and children. Key to these views is that having three places where family learning funding is likely to reside – FE literacy, language and numeracy, first steps and personal development – is likely to fragment a rich mix where the whole is greater than the parts, and exclude some valuable outcomes. There is a keen desire to see family learning of all types ring-fenced among family learning practitioners. (NIACE, 2004, p. 4)

For existing or potential learners?

The loss of 'other provision' in the college sector and the imposition of higher fees in LEAs could result in an overall drop in the number of adult learners. That in turn could reduce the range of courses available:

If there is less funding available for so-called 'leisure' courses, there will probably be fewer learners enrolling on them if they have to pay more, and then there is the obvious danger that courses that don't generate the numbers will simply be cancelled. (Sherlock, 2005, p. 19)

For new learners?

Another casualty could be the goal of widening participation in learning. Many older adults are unlikely to want narrow, qualification-focused programmes but may be unable or unwilling to pay higher fees for personal or community development programmes.

The entitlement to a free learning to achieve (a full) Level 2 qualification is unlikely to attract adults whose experience of formal learning and assessment has not been a happy one, and who, research consistently shows, are only likely to re-enter education if they can do so gradually and informally, in curriculum areas that are of immediate interest and relevance to them. It is only when confidence in learning has been achieved that many people will commit to a qualification, but they may not be prepared to do it all at once.

Moreover, despite the Skills Strategy's stress on the need to provide first step learning opportunities for adults with low skills (DfES, 2003, para. 4.39), the testimony from LLN workers and those working with people with learning difficulties suggests that the need to meet targets is actively *discouraging* providers from enrolling learners with very low skills. This means that wholly well-intentioned measures may result in a government own goal by making it difficult to attract and work with low-qualified adults who are resistant to formal education:

> *The Widening Participation agenda seems to have been forgotten, and those learners who are not capable of passing the National Test or gaining a Level 2 qualification will again lose out. I am not at all against learners working towards national qualifications, as long as they are fit for the purpose and reflect what the learner wants. But we have to be able to provide something that will attract potential learners, not just give more of the same to those already in the system.* (Lifelong Learning Co-ordinator, national voluntary organisation)

The allocation of mainstream funding to 'First Steps' provision is seen as the means of attracting such people and helping them to progress to higher-level learning.

For equal opportunities?

The raising of fees for personal and community development courses could accentuate the class divide in adult learning, whereby middle-class people who are able to afford it can engage in cultural and enrichment provision while poorer learners tend to be restricted to remedial provision such as learning to improve LLN.

Cara (1999) has pointed out that the visual arts, fitness curriculum, modern languages, local or oral history and crafts are 'the bread and butter of the curriculum offer for those who can afford to pay'. Although her comments were made in relation to the early bids received for the Adult and Community Learning Fund (ACLF), they have a particular relevance at the present time as they underline the potential consequence, in terms of reinforcing patterns of participation, of the new funding proposals:

> *Is the curriculum we are offering to those who can pay irrelevant to those who cannot? [...] Do we secretly agree that art and flower arranging, Feng Shui and flutes are leisure pursuits for the middle classes. Is provision in these areas merely a cash cow not worthy of public funding? If the answer to these questions is 'yes', then we can stop pretending that we believe in these things and devote a lot more resources to parenting skills and basic IT. If the answer is 'no', then we need to reopen our eyes to how we can offer the serious pleasures of learning in these domains to those who may not think they can afford or aspire to them.* (Cara, 1999)

For providers?

Providers could face a significant upheaval in reorganising their provision within the different funding categories, and many colleges will lose the 'other provision' that has been a substantial part of their work.

First Steps programmes will have to operate within an overarching progression strategy and in order to continue receiving funding, providers will be expected to demonstrate the effectiveness of such provision in getting learners to a point where they are ready to work towards a Level 2 qualification. To get new and unconfident learners to the point where they can undertake a full Level 2 will require a range of part-time progression routes as well as adequate time scales:

> *There will be many, of course who can sprint to the full qualification in a purposeful way. Others will take time to gain the confidence and sense of direction. For them the maintenance of a rich range of 'first steps' provision is vital.* (Tuckett, 2005)

The difficulty for providers may be the length of time it takes some learners to achieve. As a result, some may be tempted to enrol in First Steps programmes only those learners who are likely to reach the desired level, while those working with groups such as adults with learning difficulties and/or disabilities may be obliged to move provision for them to the safeguard:

> *This would certainly fit better, more logically, in terms of the provider's intention in making such provision, but, under the current proposals it will also reduce the level of funding for such provision and render the provision ineligible for additional resources for additional learning support. This could create a significant additional financial burden for providers (if they have to pick up the tab) and, longer term, discourage them from making such provision.* (NIACE, 2004)

Conversely, it has been suggested that some providers may try and shift personal development programmes aimed at new groups into First Steps provision, assuming that the funding for this will be more secure. In such cases, the need to demonstrate eventual progression could result in pressures being put on adults who have engaged in learning for reasons other than gaining a Level 2 qualification.

Another difficulty for providers may be tracking the progression of students who move from First Steps learning to higher level learning at another organisation or institution. Some organisations, especially smaller ones, have experienced problems in following up former students once they have moved on:

> *It's difficult to have a paper trail for the LSC. Knowing where people have gone to isn't always easy though we send follow-up forms. If they leave here with a Level 1 in ESOL then go on to another provider, it's the other provider that gets the credit.* (Voluntary organisation worker)

A study of learner progression from ACL has found that, apart from some information in individual learning plans, learners' next steps are not generally recorded in a form that can be collated and analysed. The time and costs involved in following up students are generally regarded as prohibitive. There are also issues around learners' willingness to respond to surveys (Cramb, 2004).

Overall, therefore, the proposals presage a significant upheaval in adult education funding, planning and organisation. Lying behind them are assumptions about what constitutes 'useful' and less useful learning, and what kinds of learning merit most public subsidy. This is not a new situation and it is not inconceivable that it heralds the resurrection in another guise of the widely disliked Schedule 2/Non-Schedule 2 curriculum division of the 1990s.[5]

The concept of 'useful' learning was prominent in Government policies during the 1990s, as reflected in the 1991 White Paper 'Education and Training for the 21st Century' which proposed the withdrawal of public funding for all but 'useful' learning. Though not carried forward in its entirety into the subsequent Further and Higher Education Act (1992), this instrumental approach provoked much discussion over the long-term and short-term utility of the outcomes from learning. (Hillage *et al.*, 2000, pp. 7–8)

---

5 Following the 1992 Further and Higher Education Act, Schedule 2 courses (accredited courses for adults, those leading to educational progression, adult literacy and LLN, English for speakers of other languages (ESOL) courses and some courses for people with learning difficulties and disabilities which could show 'progression') were funded directly by the Further Education Funding Council (FEFC). Other non-accredited 'leisure' courses were categorised as Non-Schedule 2 and responsibility for their provision was given to local education authorities. However, as the legal duty of LEAs to make 'adequate' provision was never clearly defined, some authorities reduced or dropped this kind of provision altogether and many upped their fees to cover the costs of delivering them. The distinction between these types of provision was removed in the Learning and Skills Act of 2000.

What is useful learning?

According to the Chief Inspector of Adult Learning:

The thinking behind [the funding proposals] *is that public money should only be used to fund provision which has a tangible, easily identifiable educational value.*

There is already pressure on us not to inspect ACL provision which is deemed to come under the heading 'leisure', your stereotypical evening classes in basket-weaving and yoga, for example. Yet, there are more than a million learners in the ACL sector and some 60 per cent of them do not take qualifications. The fact is that many learners don't want them – they seek personal development or community involvement. This form of learning, that is to say, non-accredited, has its own value. […]

The crux of the issue is that these aspects of human development, the non-tangible benefits of ACL, need to work doubly hard to prove that they are worthy of substantial public investment. (Sherlock, 2005, p. 19)

We have been here before. To make judgments about what constitutes useful or less useful learning perpetuates a false dichotomy that has been hanging around in post-16 education policies for decades. The distinction – in terms of learner intentions and outcomes – between different types of adult learning is not clear-cut. As has frequently been argued, to judge learner intentions and outcomes by the subject or title of a course is misleading. It ignores the fact that adults undertake different types of learning for reasons that cannot simply be labelled as 'learning for skills' or 'learning for personal development'. Courses assumed to be attended for self-development or leisure reasons are often undertaken for economic or skill-development reasons, while LLN or vocational courses are often engaged in for reasons that have nothing to do with any intention to improve skills or enhance employability.

Many people pursue formal qualifications for personal satisfaction whereas the student in the conversational Spanish class may really have an eye on applying for a job in the export section of their organisation. (Kennedy, 1997, p. 17)

There is a need to distinguish between a programme's official purpose and the purposes that individuals have for participating in such programmes. A programme may be offered for avowedly non-vocational purposes, but those participating may be doing so for vocational reasons. (LSRC, 2004, p. 43)

A research project at King's College London (Swain, 2004) found that students' motivations to take basic arithmetic were not clearly related to perceptions of 'perceived needs in employment, or to people's feelings that they have a deficit of skills in their everyday life'.

We have found it is the quality of engagement with the activity that makes the mathematics seem 'real' or meaningful and worthwhile to the learner, rather than its supposed usefulness and application in their lives outside the classroom. The implication of this finding for policy-makers is that promoting narrowly utilitarian mathematics may turn away some potential learners.

A large-scale lifelong learning survey (Eurobarometer) undertaken in 2003 in the 15 pre-2004 EU member states, Iceland and Norway, found that adults' motives for learning were often not sharply differentiated as instrumental or self-developmental, but invariably mixed. Only a minority said they undertook education and training solely for work-related or personal motives. 'Virtually all' respondents saw learning as having both work-related and personal aims and benefits, with those related to personal aspirations and outcomes being paramount (Chisholm *et al.*, 2004). This confirms the view of a number of adult education practitioners and analysts:

There is no inherent reason why people should not have economic as well as social, cultural and political goals just as they may combine individual with collective aspirations. (Mayo and Collymore, 2000)

Bhamra (2004) concludes that from the learners' perspective:

accredited and non-accredited learning are often inter-dependent and difficult to disentangle. Economic and social outcomes can be linked, just as learning can have a social and cultural purpose at the same time as leading to economic or utilitarian ends. (p. 8)

Although the current funding proposals envisage that the new system will be based on *providers'* decisions about the purposes of a programme, many argue that it is the learner's intention that should be paramount: 'It is the learner's motivation that determines whether learning is vocational or not, rather than the decision of the provider or funder' (Sargant, 2000, p. 91). Moreover, a number of studies (see, for example, Bowman *et al.*, 2000) have shown that adults' learning preferences, motivations and behaviour do not necessarily match the beliefs and assumptions of policy-makers or providers:

Many serious adult and community learners take a positive decision to shun awards. They see qualifications as a distraction from learning and an award as irrelevant to the kind of personal, career or community development they seek. (Sherlock, 2005, p. 19)

In addition, as pointed out in the ALI report (2004), the outcomes from engaging in learning may be peripheral to the original intended outcomes. Thus, as Bhamra (2004) suggests, it may be pointless to try and distinguish between the outcomes and benefits of different types of learning, as this:

can create both statistical and inferential difficulties. The differences are often ones created by funders rather than learners, for whom participation in the learning process rather than the eventual attainment is often the initial motivation. (p. 4)

The attainment that matters most to policy-makers is achievement of qualifications as a means of raising skills levels and increasing national competetiveness. The funding system is being reorganised so that the the adult learning that receives the most support is learning that leads to that end. However, the loss of wider learning opportunities that may occur in the process could have a knock-on effect, not only for individuals but also for the government's own goals. For there is evidence that a broad and comprehensive curriculum can be as, if not more, effective in meeting government priorities as provision with prescribed outcomes.

Can a broad and flexible curriculum achieve government goals?

There is a general consensus among those working in the adult education field that it can. It is widely found that 'recreational' or leisure learning plays a significant role in the government agendas of widening participation, regenerating neighbourhoods and reducing social, economic and health inequalities. These outcomes are also acknowledged in policy:

> *the government's agenda for social inclusion and its skills strategy both identify an important role for the adult and community learning* [sub-] *sector. The distinctive contribution that the sector should and can make to community cohesion, citizenship and a culture of lifelong learning is recognised.* (ALI, 2004)

What is less recognised is that non-accredited adult learning can also have direct economic benefits and, in some curriculum areas, can result in skills that have a greater chance of leading to employment than qualifications (Merton and Greenwood, 2001; Tyers and Aston, 2002; Bhamra, 2004).

Probably the greatest contribution ACL makes to government goals is its ability to engage new groups in active learning.

Widening participation

> *We need a broad and generous definition of lifelong learning in order to widen participation.* (Price, 2001, p. 12)

The literature on adult learning constantly reaffirms that the education programmes that are most effective in attracting adults and sustaining their motivation are those that respond to their interests and aspirations. Adults' first steps back into learning are often more related to their immediate priorities and concerns than to a desire for educational progression or enhanced employability. This particularly applies to groups with little tradition of engaging in lifelong learning.

> *Starting from the students' current position and building on their interests, were important features of* [interviewees'] *experiences and desires.* (Bowman *et al.*, 2000, p. 42)

This is a precondition for effective learning across the post-16 sector:

> *Students are far more likely to learn to think critically by engaging with their experience of everyday life or by becoming passionate about a book or a subject than by scrupulously attempting to achieve learning outcomes […]. Predictable and measurable outcomes have no place in an intellectually engaged environment.* (Furedi, 2004)

The NIACE (2003b) report on embedding these skills suggests that embedding these skills in subjects such as aromatherapy, family history, DIY, catering, or hair and beauty therapy is more likely than discrete *SfL* courses to attract people with poor LLN skills.

> *In 90 per cent of the research projects, the curriculum subject was the motivation to learn, not the LLN. For example, parents wanted to know how to cook nourishing meals without it costing too much; they were not motivated by the numeracy. Even in situations where there was little choice about attendance, young people on work-based learning were clear they had chosen to attend the 'literacy, language and numeracy through Creative Activities' for the various arts activities that were on offer not the literacy/language/numeracy aspects.* (NIACE, 2003a, p. 36)

Studies of family literacy have also found that it is usually the curriculum subject that creates the motivation to learn rather than a recognised need to improve LLN skills (NIACE, 2003c). Both the OFSTED (2000) survey of family learning and the NIACE (2003c) evaluation of family learning programmes in LEAs, showed that learning focused on a broader range of activities than just LLN was more successful in attracting men and families from disadvantaged and under-represented groups. The NIACE (2003c) research also found that an average of 47 per cent of learners participating in WFL were unemployed, in receipt of welfare benefits or from low-skilled groups, and an average of 20 per cent were from ethnic minority groups. Retention was found to be highest when 'a range of activities' was planned.

Research undertaken in Lancashire (Horne and Haggart, 2004) also indicates that WFL is more likely to result in learner progression to further learning or other activities than FLLN. Just under 60 per cent of parents who participated in WFL attributed at least one of their next step activities to taking part in it, compared with 40 per cent of those who participated in FLLN. Twenty-four per cent of WFL learners compared with 15 per cent of FLLN learners went on to enter FE or job-training programmes, while 18 per cent of WFL learners compared with 8 per cent of FLLN learners became classroom assistants.

Family learning involving a range of activities such as music, creative arts and sport often incorporates a focus on improving LLN skills. The NIACE (2003c) research found that despite a dearth of quantitative evidence, there was some consensus that WFL makes a contribution to meeting *SfL* targets by acting as a 'gateway' through

31

which people enter lifelong learning: '[It] can keep people involved in learning until they feel ready and able to move on' (Horne, 2004, p. 21).

Given these outcomes, government and policy-makers should be provided with evidence that broad and balanced learning provision plays an important role in re-engaging adults in learning and helping them to progress (Lamb, 2004).

Progression

A large number of studies, both quantitative and qualitative, have also demonstrated the role of general adult education programmes in stimulating further learning (see, for example, Bhamra, 2004; Janssen, 2004; McGivney, 1994; 1995; 2001; Morrell *et al.*, 2004).

A classic example of how learning based on personal interests, enthusiasms and curiosity can lead to educational progression is provided by the pioneering Employee Development Assistance Programme (EDAP) at Ford. Evaluations of the programme have indicated that the opportunity to engage in non-work-related learning activities of their choice has led many employees, including manual workers and individuals with no previous experience of post-16 learning, to move into more formal education programmes:

> *At first people learned to drive, to play golf, went on weekend courses to find out how to run a pub. Within three years people were studying languages, computing or signed up on Open University courses. As many blue collar workers as white collar workers took up the project, and over the years it has extended to offer opportunities for workers' families [...] EDAP was showing the value of learning for its own sake just as public bodies were becoming convinced that education for pleasure had little right to public subsidy. (Tuckett, 2001)*

Research supplies a number of other examples. A DfES survey of learners involved in non-accredited learning in 2001–02 (Morrell *et al.*, 2004) showed that two-thirds went on to do further learning in 2002–03.

The evaluation of Schedule 2 pilots (Merton and Greenwood, 2001) showed that a significant number of the 28,377 reported participants in 1999–2000 stayed in learning and went on to enrol in both accredited and other non-accredited programmes.

An evaluation of the education projects supported by the ACLF found that they were: 'particularly effective at getting people into learning, enhancing their soft skills, and engaging their interest for learning and progression in the future' (Tyers and Aston, 2002, p. 42).

Family learning programmes focused on a range of subjects such as foreign languages, football, digital technology and the creative arts have been found to motivate adults to consider engaging in more formal courses including those aimed at improving LLN skills (Horne, 2004; NIACE, 2003c).

These examples suggest that courses that may soon fall within the category of 'personal and community development' rather than 'First Steps' learning often themselves act as first steps back into sustained learning for many adults:

> *It is possible to see any and every entry point into learning as having the potential to build into longer term, more ambitious engagement.* (London Skills Commission, 2004, quoted in Bhamra, 2004)

The Skills Strategy (DfES, 2003) has acknowledged that many adults need to engage in less formal programmes before gaining the confidence to undertake higher level and accredited learning, and this has been the rationale for proposing a first steps strategy as a means of easing people back into learning.

> *There are some* [people] *with low skills who would welcome opportunities to improve their skills but would feel daunted by full qualifications. They want a 'first step' on the learning ladder before committing themselves. Reaching such reluctant learners is an important part of achieving our aims.* (DfES, 2003, para. 4.39)

However, there are many routes back into learning. Creating a specific first steps category could leave much of the 'other provision' that already acts as a first step for many adults vulnerable if the funding safeguard is inadequate to support it, and if it is offered at a fee that some adults cannot afford.

Neighbourhood renewal and social inclusion

Appealing to people's immediate interests is a well-established way of stimulating local involvement and activism. Policy Action Team 10, in its report *Successful Participation for All*, recommended 'using the arts, sport and leisure to engage people in poor neighbourhoods, particularly those who feel most excluded' (PAT 10, 1999, p. 28, para. 1.6).

Learning involving such activities can bring about significant improvements in community attitudes and behaviour. Examples of this have been observed following participation in WFL programmes. One school in special measures which had developed an effective arts programme involving families, reported a significant transformation of the culture of the school and, 'a miraculous change round in the attitude of the local community towards school' (NIACE, 2003c, p. 114).

Other schools with WFL activities have also reported better relationships with parents and a better atmosphere within schools. In one school they had helped staff to 'work towards making the school a more inclusive environment.' In another, four participants on a WFL course had gone on to become school governors:

> *Many parents were developing skills that had enabled them to take a more active part in their communities. One of the parents taking part in the money management programme had become active in the local credit union that was run from the school.*

> *In another session observed, a parent described how the course she had attended had helped to give her the confidence to tackle the problems in her neighbourhood. 'I've been able to write a letter to my Housing Association about the abandoned cars in the area. I got a petition going and everyone signed it.'*

> *Another learner had gained the confidence to be part of a delegation of parents who lobbied the Chief Executive of a local authority about what was needed in the neighbourhood.* (NIACE, 2003c, pp. 114–5)

Community involvement of this kind is an important element in community cohesion and neighbourhood regeneration, both of which are important goals of the current government. Improving skills for citizenship is part of the social inclusion agenda and one of the national priorities included in the LSC guidance on Adult Learning Plans (LSC, 2003–04). Although there are differing views on the interpretation of citizenship, a literature review of a wide range of studies revealed a significant link between the concept and participation in less formal and 'almost invariably non-accredited' learning (Bhamra, 2004). Studies of citizenship such as Coare and Johnston (2003) and Preston (2004) found that informal learning was the 'key' to an engagement with citizenship.

Particularly robust evidence comes from quantitative analysis of the longitudinal Child Development Study. This indicated that although the impact on active citizenship is not always immediate:

> *taking courses between the ages of 33 and 42 predicted greater levels of civic and political participation.* **The effects were largest in relation to taking leisure courses. The effects of taking leisure courses on civic participation were particularly strong for those with below Level 2 qualifications at age 33.** [My emphasis] (Schuller *et al.*, 2004, p. 155)

Schuller *et al.*'s *Benefits of Learning* report also demonstrated that attendance at adult education 'leisure' courses had positively increased tolerance, understanding and respect for others, all of which are essential ingredients of community cohesion.

Health and well-being

The positive impact participation in enjoyable and stimulating learning has on individual self-confidence and self-esteem is mentioned in most research on the benefits of learning (see Aldridge and Lavender, 1999; Bhamra, 2004; Eldred *et al.*, 2005; James and Nightingale, 2004; McGivney, 1995; 2003).

The positive impact learning any subject 'from computing to logic, from bridge to singing' (Janssen, 2004) can have on health is also reasserted frequently in research (see, for example, Bhamra, 2004; James, 2001a; 2001b; 2004; Schuller *et al.*, 2004).

These are important findings for those who consider learning that is not related to qualifications to be intrinsically less valuable and less worthy of public investment than learning that does lead to such outcomes.

> *The contribution that non-accredited ACL programmes can make, and are making, to community cohesion, social inclusion, citizenship and a culture of lifelong learning – all national government priorities – should be fully recognised. And we will say as much when we submit our response to the LSC's proposals.* (Sherlock, 2005, p. 19)

The range of outcomes resulting from participation in ACL programmes are ostensibly recognised in policy as evinced by the ongoing RARPA project.[6] They are stated very clearly in the Five-Year Strategy White Paper (DfES, 2004):

> *Skills and learning are not just about economic goals. They are also about the pleasure of learning for its own sake, the dignity of self-improvement and the achievement of personal potential.*
>
> *Research shows that such learning has a positive impact in many different ways; on the individual and their sense of purpose, motivation, health and well being; on their family and on their children's learning; and on society and the individual's involvement in the wider community. They help people build the confidence to come back into learning, offering the first step to qualifications for those who want them.* (DfES, 2004, p. 25)

However valuable these outcomes are ostensibly believed to be, they are still, and increasingly, subordinated to the twin goals of qualifications and employability. In some cases this has resulted in two interrelated policy aims – raising skill levels and widening participation in learning – pulling in opposite directions. A voluntary

---

6 RARPA stands for Recognising and Recording Progress and Achievement in non-accredited learning. It is a means of validating the outcomes of programmes which do not result in qualifications or other outcomes certified by awarding bodies. The LSC aims to adopt RARPA as an underlying quality assurance process for non-accredited learning in 2005/06.

There are two elements to the RARPA approach:

1) The *staged process*, consisting of five core steps which provide a means of recording progress and achievement for non-accredited learning.
2) *Quality assurance processes* for RARPA which use providers' existing self-assessment and continuous improvement processes.

organisation which has been warned by the LSC that the courses it offers do not make sufficient contribution to *SfL* targets is, at the same time, frequently held up as a model of good practice in widening participation and invited to give presentations at national events:

> *It's a contradictory situation. On the one hand people say we want more voluntary sector organisations in order to widen participation; on the other they don't give you any credit for doing that. It's a continual battle.*

There also seems to be a tragic loss of emphasis on social exclusion and community development in the current thrust of policy, with no apparent connection between the economic and social exclusion agendas. It is frequently observed that the wide-ranging benefits of learning are less appreciated in the DfES than in other government departments. However, as Flint (2005) points out: 'We ignore the extra-ordinary social payback from adult learning in health, family life and community development at our peril' (p. 25).

Current policies tend to be based on the learning adults are assumed to want or need and take little account of their *actual* choices and preferences. Where, for example, is the match between the Level 2 entitlement and adults' own, expressed learning aspirations?

The emphasis on 'listening to learners' that has been a feature of policy documents since the late 1990s, appears to be diminishing.

Are we listening to learners?

Too often we prescribe the boundaries of the learning on offer too narrowly. As one student in a literacy class for adults with learning difficulties told my colleague Jeannie Sutcliffe a decade ago, 'I want to learn about Jesus and history, and thunder and lightning.' (Tuckett, 2001)

Providers, practitioners, researchers, and indeed policy-makers themselves, frequently stress the importance of listening to what learners actually want. There is widespread consensus that a curriculum that responds to the expressed interests, wishes and needs of learners is more effective in sustaining their motivation and encouraging learning success than one that has imposed content and pre-determined outcomes. Guidance and case studies of good practice for providers of learning opportunities for adults therefore usually recommend that learners be allowed to play a part in planning and designing the curriculum.

The evaluation of Non-Schedule 2 pilots (Merton and Greenwood, 2001) found that where learners had been involved in the design of their curriculum, there was a clear commitment to its success, a sense of ownership of the learning activities, and a determination in some instances to sustain the life of the learning groups beyond the involvement of the learning provider.

A comparison of widening participation initiatives in Sweden and the UK found that the projects that were most successful in engaging learners were those that had not made assumptions about what learners wanted or needed but involved active interaction between learners and provider:

The experience from the UK and Sweden showed that learning programmes for 'hard-to-reach' groups work best when the content was demand-led and based on what the learners themselves were interested in. For each of the projects, developing an enabling curriculum meant incorporating the life experiences, history, contributions and perspectives of all students in the content and delivery of each subject area. This requires an understanding of the learners that could only be gained by listening to them. (NIACE and Foreign and Commonwealth Office, 2003, p. 31)

Among the factors for success identified in the UK and Sweden study were: not making assumptions about learners' needs; listening to them; starting with something relevant to them; and recognising the value of learning which may appear 'useless.'

Cavanagh's (2000) exploration of different approaches to the curriculum concludes that one which focuses on the interests, wishes, needs and abilities of the individual is the most inclusive and 'purest' form of curriculum organisation:

> *Each learner is unique. They learn at differing rates, they scan the knowledge base differently extracting from it those parts that they can incorporate into their learning frame, implicitly rejecting some knowledge as too difficult, too far removed from the immediacy of the problem to be solved, not applicable to their particular stage of intellectual, social, physical, emotional development, boring or at the very least uninteresting and so on. The knowledge about learners under this design must form a critical platform for decisions about the curriculum. Such knowledge must be made explicit and used as the guiding principle for curriculum development.* (Cavanagh, 2000, pp. 38–9)

This corresponds to the views of many people working in ACL.

One area where the principle of responding to individual learner interests and needs is strongly advocated is work with people with learning difficulties and/or disabilities. Smith (2004), for example, endorses the inclusive, person-centred approach set out in the Department of Health report, *Valuing People* (2000), in which the focus of planning shifts away from services and towards the needs, dreams and aspirations of the individual:

> *The process is essentially about enabling individuals to have more control over their own lives. Education has a role to play in supporting learners towards the achievement of their person-centred plan by taking full account of their expressed aspirations. Person-centred plans should guide the development of an appropriate programme.*
>
> *If we continue to 'decide what's best for learners' we will continue to miss those opportunities to develop self-esteem, skills of assertiveness and problem-solving which enable increasing learner autonomy and independence in the community. Choice and a sense of control over one's own life give life meaning, purpose and joy.* (Smith, 2004, pp. 30–1)

Case studies in the Qualifications and Curriculum Authority (QCA) guidance on developing a learner-centred curriculum for young adults with learning difficulties (QCA, 2002) illustrate how individual learners have been able to follow a diverse range of programmes that support their varied wishes and aspirations. The aim of the person-centred plan advocated in the guidance is to find ways of meeting personal goals rather than trying to fit individuals into existing provision: 'Person-centred planning works from a value base that shifts the power of professionals and carers from that of power over the person to power alongside them' (Maudslay and Nightingale, 2004, p. 18).

Other research with people with learning difficulties and/or disabilities (Anderson *et al.*, 2005) also emphasises the importance of listening to students and responding to what they say in order to design an appropriate curriculum: 'Many discrete learning programmes fail to match students' requirements and aspirations as they are insufficiently tailored to individuals' (Anderson *et al.*, 2005, p. 39).

Choice and flexibility are also considered important elements in the design of a curriculum for young people:

> *Most* [working in this field] *argue that young adults should be given choice: that provision and programmes should be negotiated with young people; that where possible activities should be converted into learning and that it is up to the young adults as to whether that should be accredited or not. That is the premise upon which the Getting Connected programme is offered.* (Development Officer in national organisation)

Learners' preferences

The LSC *National Learner Satisfaction Survey* (LSC, 2004b) found that the highest levels of satisfaction were expressed by learners participating in a range of non-accredited learning. Moreover, as seen earlier, there is substantial evidence that many adults prefer a wider curriculum to a narrow one that focuses on specific accreditation targets:

> *If ACL is about encouraging more people to come back to learning, especially those who did not have good experiences at school, then we must understand why learners choose the course that they do. The intention of a provider when running a course may be a lot different from the intentions of the learners who enrol on it. As we now know, many learners are looking for benefits aside from qualifications.* (Sherlock, 2005, p. 19)

Research and practice indicate that adults with poor basic skills or learning difficulties, as well as those involved in family learning, often have purposes broader than the improvement of LLN when they engage in learning. The NIACE (2003a) report on embedding LLN proposes that the interests and needs arising from leisure, work or personal interests should become more prominent in curriculum design and delivery.

Chisholm *et al.* (2003) claim that the most effective family learning provision includes opportunities across the curriculum, including subjects such as sport, local history and music. There is evidence of unmet demand for such learning.

> *The NIACE evaluation* [of family learning in LEAs] *highlighted that the demand for wider family learning programmes is much higher in some LEAs than can be provided, ironic as many delegates reported that they were unable to recruit enough parents within the tight definitions of FLLN programmes.* (Savitsky, 2004)

To meet demand, the NIACE report on family learning in local authorities recommends that links be made with more areas of the national curriculum, for example science, languages and history, and that the curriculum should be broadened to include the arts, popular culture, sport and leisure, and neighbourhood issues, as well as parenting education. This would have a greater appeal for groups underrepresented in family learning such as men, older learners and ethnic minority communities (NIACE, 2003c, p. 132).

Lochrie (2005) also calls for a broader overall family learning curriculum, suggesting that it should include, in addition to LLN, ESOL and ICT, topics such as children's development, health and nutrition, home–school links, foundation and key stage development, practical skills for families in relation to domestic finance, tax and benefits, employment, housing, health and education, and skills and knowledge linking families to local regeneration and capacity-building initiatives.

There have also been calls to broaden the educational offer in prisons. The All-Party Parliamentary Group for Further Education and Lifelong Learning (2004) includes in its list of recommendations, that:

- *There should be significant additional investment in work-related training, and in academic, and other learning opportunities for the more able and/or longer-term prisoners;*
- *Progress in 'embedding' basic and work skills training in practical and creative courses should be extended;*
- *The value of general interest and arts-based courses in developing self-esteem and motivation to get back on track should be formally recognized;*
- *Work-related learning and training at least equal to that available in the community be made available to all in prison.*

(All-Party Parliamentary Group for Further Education and Lifelong Learning, 2004, p. 4).

· · · · ·

All stakeholders in the field of adult education it seems – learners, providers, practitioners and researchers – are calling for a broad and balanced range of learning programmes to be offered to adults. But is anyone listening?

Listening and responding to learners and potential learners is a stated aim of policy and has been written into the LSC's remit. One of the principles on which Local Learning Plans are based is 'placing learner need at the heart of planning' (DfEE, 2000b). Subsequent documents, however, suggest that it is employers' rather than learners' needs that are paramount. In its annual statement of priorities (LSC, 2004c), the first one listed is: 'Make learning truly demand-led so that it better meets the needs of employers, young people and adults' (an order that suggests a hierarchy of precedence), and while there is a mention of 'a duty to support social inclusion' on the first page, there is no further allusion to this. (It has also been noticed that social inclusion is disappearing from the action plans being produced by Regional Skills Partnerships.) The annual statement speaks mainly of employers' needs and skills gaps. Although individual needs are mentioned, they are seen largely as employment needs. But what *are* employers' needs?

What are employers' needs?

Ivan Lewis, Minister for Adult Skills and Vocational Education, has articulated the government's position very clearly:

> *We will certainly always protect learning for learning's sake, learning for quality of life, learning for leisure, but the state subsidy for that will be less than it is for skills for employability. No apologies for that and I think it's right not just in terms of economic success but also right in terms of social justice.* (Lewis, 2004, p. 13)

But do we know what constitutes 'employability'?

According to a report from the Learning and Skills Research Centre (2004), employers differ widely in the way they interpret the term and in what they want from their workers:

> *Policy documents and public commentary offer analyses and statements about 'what employers want' without often considering that employers' views are not uniform. Skill needs differ by sector or by region. Some employers are satisfied with job entrants who have literacy, language and numeracy, as they will train them to suit their needs.*

> *Variability in 'what employers want' can be seen in the disappointing take-up of some initiatives. Many employers appear uninterested in apprenticeship, particularly those in sectors without this tradition and where there is not a strong demand for Level 3 skills.* (The Learning and Skills Research Centre, 2004, p. 26)

Although the belief that employability equates with the holding of qualifications may be confirmed at the higher qualification levels, research suggests that the economic benefits of lower qualifications can be exaggerated. Even the latest Skills White Paper (DfES, 2005) includes data showing that there is no significant wage return from gaining vocational qualifications at Levels 1 and 2, except when the Level 2 is gained through the workplace.

Similarly, quantitative analyses of longitudinal research results conducted for the Wider Benefits of Learning Research Centre produced what is described as an 'intriguing finding':

Vocational courses leading to qualifications led to very few quality of life and social capital benefits. Vocational qualifications obtained between [ages] 33 and 42 have no identifiable wage returns. (Schuller *et al.*, 2004, p. 176)

An analysis of the 2001 Skills Survey (Felstead *et al.*, 2002) showed that while there were 5.3 million people qualified at Level 2, only 3.9 million jobs required a highest qualification at this level. Moreover, the number of jobs requiring no qualifications (6.5 million) considerably exceeded the number of people of working age without qualifications (2.9 million).

The survey confirms that simply supplying increasing numbers of qualifications is unlikely to be the full answer to raising the skills that are exercised in British workplaces. [...] The 'excess supply' sits oddly alongside reports of continued recruitment difficulties faced by employers and ongoing reports of skills gaps. This apparent paradox is resolved once it is recalled that qualifications are often only loose indicators of the skills actually required at work. (Felstead *et al.*, 2002, p. 78–9)

Citing the work of Michael Eraut at the University of Sussex, the Learning and Skills Research Centre (2004) report on vocational learning makes a similar point, noting that there can be a difference between obtaining a qualification and being skilled or qualified to do a particular job:

Policy targets are often expressed in terms of attainment of qualifications, which represents only a small subset of acquired learning and competence. NVQs, for example, measure a portion of on-the-job learning and, by design, separate assessment of on-the-job learning from work-related learning in educational settings. Attaining the qualification has become the mark of success, which is not the same as being qualified for a job, as job performance is context-specific. (p. 28)

And later in the same document:

It is important to remember that achievement of a Level 3 qualification is not the same as being prepared for Level 3 work, and that achieving the qualification may not guarantee an ability to perform well on the job. (p. 32)

It is also clear from research that many adults do not share the assumption that learning for a qualification automatically enhances their employment chances or work performance. Community-based research (Bowman *et al.*, 2000) found that respondents did not see clear links between educational achievement and work opportunities. Their experience was that the range of work opportunities available to them was often limited, that qualifications were not always valued and recognised, and that employers often discriminated arbitrarily against certain applicants and appointed people for reasons other than their qualifications:

In our study interviewees believed that employers often recruited on some other basis than qualifications, namely experience or through personal networks, or using some idiosyncratic notion of personal qualities, and that they did not necessarily value certain qualifications at all.

Some of the people interviewed during the research did not consider that education and training was the preferred route to employment. Others had found through their experiences of participating in government schemes that the opportunities actually open to them differed significantly from those claimed by policy-makers, education providers and benefit advisors. (Bowman *et al.*, 2000, pp. 38–9)

These findings led the researchers to conclude that assumptions about the link between qualifications and jobs have little to do with the realities of many people's experience, although the link is taken as a given in policy.

Informal workplace learning

Another significant research finding is that employees find informal learning at work more useful than training and qualifications in developing the key skills demanded by many employers, such as communication skills, problem-solving and team-working. In their survey of 1,943 employees in 2004, Felstead *et al.* (2005) discovered that training courses and the acquisition of qualifications were lowly rated by respondents in terms of their helpfulness in enhancing work performance. One in four employees reported that training courses were of little or no value in improving work performance and about one in three thought that studying for qualifications had not helped them at work:

Activities more closely associated with the workplace – such as doing the job, being shown things, engaging in self-reflection and keeping one's eyes and ears open – were reckoned to provide more helpful insights into how to do the job better. All of these factors were rated as more helpful sources of learning than attending training courses or acquiring qualifications. (Felstead *et al.*, 2005, p. 8)

Similar findings come from Ireland: 'The development of soft skills is a measure of success and a pre-requisite to long-term and successful work. Too many agencies are target-driven' (Paddy Richardson, Co-ordinator of Employability Programmes, Business in the Community).[7]

It is argued that the importance of soft skills in workplace performance also applies to management training:

---

7 Comment made in an address made at the *Reaching Out* seminar held in Limerick on 22 February 2005).

It would be easy to assume that a focus on deliverables [in management training] *equates to a focus on technical, measurable skills. But both consultants and university experts say it's exactly the opposite: that the emphasis is on 'soft skills' such as team working and leadership.* [According to an executive director of a consultancy] *there is more of an emphasis on things like emotional intelligence and relationship management.* (Plimmer, 2004, p. 3)

Economic outcomes

Although many non-accredited learning programmes result in the acquisition of 'soft skills' such as communication skills, problem-solving, team-work and presentation skills, suggestions that there can be a link between informal learning and economic activity are often treated with scepticism. The Learning and Skills Research Centre report (2004) makes the point that the lack of evidence on the economic benefits from participating in non-accredited ACL (a common argument used to justify its lower perceived value) is partly because qualifications – the normal proxies used for skills in estimating rates of return – are traditionally not a major feature of this kind of provision.

Yet there is some evidence that learning that does not ostensibly lead to qualifications or jobs can be linked to economic activity. A survey of 900 learners participating in part-time, non-accredited courses in arts, crafts and modern languages found that many of them were using their new skills to improve their employment prospects or to help in their current employment. A number of those learning modern foreign languages were doing so for job-related reasons, while in virtually all of the arts and crafts courses surveyed, there were learners who were taking commissions, selling their work and starting small businesses (McGivney, 1994; 1995).

Participation in WFL has also helped some adults to gain paid employment:

A tutor interviewed described how she had started as a learner on a [wider] *family learning course herself years before. She had progressed through several programmes, gaining confidence, and had eventually gained her qualification for teaching adults. She was now a valued member of the Family Learning Team. Another of the parents interviewed had become a childminder as a result of wider family learning programmes attended.* (NIACE, 2003c, p. 115)

Such outcomes often result from participation in ACL, but they are not systematically recorded by providers or recognised by funding agencies intent only on meeting specific qualification targets. One voluntary organisation that offers a range of education and training courses for women has 'a good record of getting women into employment but the LSC doesn't take account of this'. This is despite the stress on 'employability' in policy.

There appears, therefore, to be a disjuncture between what is being said and what is actually happening. In consequence, the stated aim of government for education and training to be 'demand-led' is treated with scepticism by some commentators:

> *You can't wade very far into official further education prose these days before you bump into 'demand led'. The tag is everywhere in directives from the Department for Education and Skills and the assorted quangos and agencies and it pops up in every other ministerial speech.*

> *Among the 'major challenges' listed in the government's recent progress report on its own skills strategy was the need to 'convince both employers and learners that we are making a reality of a demand-led, responsive approach to delivering training.' But whose demand is it anyway?* (Kingston, 2004b)

Most policy documents suggest that the only 'demand' (usually interpreted as skill shortages) that is really taken into consideration is that of employers and the labour market, while learning provision for which there *is* an obvious demand (from adults themselves) is being reduced or cut altogether:

> *Although there is a demand for these courses (e.g. leisure learning courses), colleges may have to reduce subsidies on them and start charging learners and employers.* (LSRC, 2004, p. 28)

> *Demand-led somehow suggests that colleges have radically altered the way they operate. That they used to put on courses merely to please themselves but from now on they are going to take the bother to find out what the punters actually want.*

> *But does it really mean that? Ask the thousand or so punters at Bradford College who were enjoying their yoga, tai chi, swimming and other adult education "physical health" classes, whether they demanded that the courses suddenly be scrapped this autumn.*

> *Or ask deaf students about the £138 fee that Macclesfield College is slapping on their lip-reading class, which has hitherto been free. Or ask the thousands of people in and around Bristol who fear the dismantling of that city's adult and community education service in its present form. Indeed, ask adult students all over the country how reassured they are by this new demand-led mode of operations.* (Kingston, 2004b)

Where, in all this, is the vision?

Where is the vision?

There is almost no vision in the system as it is now. There is a preoccupation with targets, goals and short-term cost-effectiveness. [...]

Lifelong education is about more than the acquisition of certificates. Participants in learning look for both vocational training and education for health, the environment, social and community needs, and for recreational leisure. These are essential parts of modern living. For many adults, young, in mid-life, and those retired [...] the broad education these areas offer may well represent the difference between independence and dependence in old age. It is the sharp narrowing of opportunities for such liberal education provided by the public education service that is bringing most forms of adult community education, including that in residential colleges, to their knees. (Gilbert, 2004, p. 21)

Since David Blunkett's much-quoted preface to the *The Learning Age* (DfEE, 1998)[8] there have been frequent reaffirmations of the broad role and value of learning. At the beginning of the twenty-first century, the vision of a rich lifelong learning culture was still embedded in policy and written into the remit of the newly established LSC:

Not all learning should lead to awards. Many adults, including large numbers of older and retired learners, will want to pursue high quality and rigorous study for its own sake and I expect provision to be made available to meet their needs. (Blunkett, 2000)

The maintenance of a balanced curriculum offer for adults was also made a duty of Local Learning Partnerships, with Local Learning Plans required to:

ensure that adults should have a wide curriculum with a balance between recreational, academic and vocational learning, learning for personal and family growth (including basic and key skills) and learning to enhance the capacity of communities. (DfEE, 2000b)

---

8 'As well as securing our economic future, learning has a wider contribution. It helps make ours a civilised society, develops the spiritual side of our lives and promotes active citizenship. Learning enables people to play a full part in their community. It strengthens the family, the neighbourhood and consequently the nation. It helps us fulfil our potential and opens doors to a love of music, art and literature. That is why we value learning for its own sake as well as for the equality of opportunity it brings.' (DfEE, 1998)

More recently, despite its overall emphasis on raising skill levels, the Skills Strategy has reasserted the requirement for adults to be offered:

> *a broad range of opportunities for those who get pleasure and personal fulfilment from learning. A civilised society should provide opportunities to enable everyone, including those who have retired, to learn for its own sake.* (DfES, 2003, para. 4.40)

The Five-Year Strategy White Paper *Access to Learning for All* (DfES, 2004) reiterates these sentiments:

> *Skills and learning are not just about economic goals. They are also about the pleasure of learning for its own sake, the dignity of self-improvement and the achievement of personal potential.* (DfES, 2004, p. 24)

In reality, if not in the intention, however, there has already been a retreat from the spirit of this declaration:

> *Six years on from Blunkett's Preface the dynamic for widening participation is at best stalled. The commitment to learning for citizenship, for personal and community development has weakened and once again we inhabit a policy environment dominated by short-term utilitarian skills needs.* (Tuckett, 2004)

The intensifying bias towards investment in adult learning that is explicitly related to qualifications, skills and employment (DfES, 2005) is worrying. Although there is a commitment to protect non-accredited areas of the curriculum and the funding safeguard will secure a proportion of it in the short term, the range and richness of adult learning provision is already under threat as LLSCs attempt to meet the priorities set out in the Skills Strategy – learners aged 16–19, adult LLN and the Level 2 entitlement (for which no extra funds have been made available) (LSC, 2004c).

Once again, a strongly instrumental view of learning prevails in policy, with learning leading to qualifications and enhanced employability given clear priority over learning undertaken for other reasons. Although it is recognised that learning for citizenship, reduction of poverty and social cohesion also merits public funding, the overall emphasis is very firmly on labour market objectives. The policy position is that the most important role of learning is to get people back into work and this goal is being pursued at the expense of learning for other purposes. Many working in the field of adult education consider this to be retrogressive and extremely unfortunate:

> *A hierarchy of importance […], in which job-related learning is continually privileged over other forms, risks not only misunderstanding what motivates many adults to learn but also missing the Government's own goals of strengthening communities and families. This orientation also fails to take account of the complexity of the relationship between learning and the economy and the sad experience of successive Government-*

sponsored training schemes in the folk memory of many deprived communities.
(Fullick, 2004, p. 5)

The current government priorities are made explicit in the title and content of the White Paper *Skills: Getting On in Business, Getting On at Work,* published in March 2005, which outlines policies and progress in improving adult education and skills. Nevertheless, like earlier policy documents, the Paper makes explicit and persuasive reference to learning for leisure and personal development:

> *There are millions of people in this country who pursue training and skills not for any job related purpose but for personal development, civic and social engagement, pleasure and interest. That includes millions of people who have retired and others sustaining the fabric of family and community life. While the economic and vocational purposes of skills are vital, they are in no sense the whole story. A cultured and civilised society must also sustain a wide range of opportunities to gain skills and acquire knowledge for their own intrinsic value. Investment in personal and community learning secures health and citizenship benefits for individuals and communities.*
> (DfES, 2005, para. 231)

The day after the White Paper's publication, however, a parliamentary question to the Secretary of State for Education and Skills about measures 'to improve provision of adult education' elicited only in response a list of policies on skills and training: the creation of Sector Skills Councils and Employer Training Pilots, 'both of which create a powerful new employer-led direction to skills provision'; the roll-out of the National Employer Training Programme; the creation of new Skills Academies; the roll-out of the Level 2 entitlement; and the development of an extended careers, training and support service (NIACE, 2005a). Apart from the Level 2 entitlement, there was no reference in the response either to adults or to education. The 'millions of people' learning for other purposes mentioned in the paragraph quoted are presumably judged to be fully catered for.

Although the term is still occasionally (if infrequently) used in policy documents, the concept of 'lifelong learning' appears to have shrunk to a focus on giving people, mostly younger adults, the skills required by employers. This seems to be a Europe-wide phenomenon. It is only a few years since the goal of lifelong learning was receiving prominent emphasis in European education policy. Now there appears to be a steady retreat from that objective:

> *One of the main reasons why the Commission's Memorandum on Lifelong Learning (2000) was warmly welcomed by Member States, was that it finally acknowledged the importance of learning for personal fulfilment and for democratic citizenship as the necessary second and third pillar of lifelong learning policies for lifelong learning, alongside the vocational training component. In many countries, these areas had tended to be neglected in educational policy development in the preceding years.*

Reports [...] suggest that most Member States may be withdrawing more and more from funding the traditional institutional framework and the human resources which are so vital for adult education for personal fulfilment and democratic citizenship and for sustaining or creating 'enabling lifelong learning environments'. (Commission of the European Communities, 2004, 1.2.1 and 1.2.2)

The emphasis on education's role in developing skills and preparing individuals for the labour market has already had a marked impact on the extent and nature of ACL provision in this country. As seen earlier, some LLSCs have already advised providers to concentrate on Skills Strategy priorities and some LSC-funded institutions and organisations have already dropped certain courses and programmes in the expectation of withdrawal of funding from those that do not contribute to the national targets.

The actual and expected erosion of the richness of the curriculum offer is preoccupying both practitioners and others working with or on behalf of adults, many of whom feel that the *SfL* targets and Level 2 entitlement are being pursued at the expense of everything else. There are major concerns about the extent to which the curriculum is being skewed, and those with the lowest skills excluded, so that providers can meet local targets. However, as encountered in the collection of evidence for this paper, many practitioners do not want to go public with their complaints for fear of incurring the displeasure of LLSCs or institutional managers:

Some heads of department are toeing the government line although they're aware of disquiet among staff. Some practitioners are very distressed at the way funding is going but are reluctant to go public because of pressure within their college. It's a touchy subject that some don't want to talk about. (Development Officer, national organisation)

This is not to discount the wholly laudable intentions behind *SfL*; the massive investment in it and its impressive successes in raising LLN levels. However, it is ironic that targets that aim to raise overall skills levels are having the perverse effect of discouraging the participation of learners with the lowest skills levels due to the LSC's and providers' anxiety to meet public service agreement (PSA) targets. This is a regrettable consequence of the general audit culture which affects public services and which could undermine the whole lifelong learning/widening participation enterprise.

It is also ironic that at the same time as the curriculum for adults appears to be shrinking in response to policy directions, the curriculum in compulsory education is beginning to open up! In its annual survey of trends in education, NFER (2004) reports that one of the key aims of *Excellence and Enjoyment – A Strategy for Primary Schools* launched in 2003, was to 'empower primary schools to take control of their curriculum, and to be more innovative and to develop their own character.' The survey also reports that the majority of head teachers would like to include more time on creative subjects, to do more cross-curricular work, and to have greater flexibility in the curriculum (NFER, 2004, p. 7). Many working in adult education would echo these sentiments.

It should be acknowledged, however, that the LSC is in a difficult situation. The Learning and Skills legislation of 2000 prioritised services for young people aged 14–19 but specified only 'reasonable' provision for adults. Given that not all adult learning can be subsidised at a time of dwindling resources, the challenge the LSC faces is how to meet the priorities set out in the Skills Strategy as well as support adult learning that falls outside them:

> *Demand can be limitless, but resources are finite and we have to choose where we invest public money to achieve our targets, deliver the skills employers and individuals need, and realise the nation's ambitions to compete with the best in the world.* (LSC, 2004a)

The compromise is the safeguard, which, on the face of it, is a fair and sensible way of protecting wider adult learning. However, there are concerns about the adequacy of the safeguard budget to support the number of 'other' programmes that may be shifted to it in order to accommodate *SfL*, First Steps and Level 2 provision. There is an obvious danger that in concentrating on these priority areas, many providers will shift other provision to what may end up being a very small resource.

Whatever happens, it is likely that the volume and diversity of adult provision will continue to be eroded, and there will continue to be constraints on creative curriculum development. As pointed out by the Learning and Skills Research Centre (2004), overemphasis on targets linked to qualifications can detract from considerations related to the design and appropriateness of learning programmes.

Loss of momentum towards wider participation

Adult learners are extremely diverse. They have been described by Turner with Tuckett (2003, p. 2) as:

> *people of all ages from 16 upwards, with equally variable motivations, backgrounds, experiences and capabilities. They include those with little or no adult learning experience through to those with advanced degrees, adults with literacy, numeracy and ESOL needs and those with learning difficulties and disabilities.*

The literature on adult learning consistently shows that a curriculum that is based on the varied interests and wishes of learners is far more effective in attracting new learners and sustaining their motivation than one that is imposed and has pre-determined outcomes. There is considerable evidence, for example, that in different areas of adult education – LLN, family learning, work with adults with learning difficulties – the stimulus to engage in learning usually stems from wider personal interests rather than a recognised need to improve literacy or other key skills. It is becoming more widely recognised that harnessing such interests can lead to engagement in learning and learning success (Casey, 2005).

The opportunity to participate in a non-accredited course that meets their interests gives people the confidence to know that they can learn and is often the starting point for a lifelong engagement with learning. In the 2002–03 *National Learner Satisfaction Survey* (LSC, 2004b), 69 per cent of learners on non-accredited ACL courses felt more confident in their ability to learn.

To allow wider adult learning to wither on the vine in pursuit of targets suggests a fundamental misunderstanding of what actually brings people into learning:

> *What is being lost is the recognition that adult learning is triggered by interest, curiosity, pleasure, unfulfilled desire – a sense that 'there must be something more' to life in ways that might make a real difference. It is made possible by free and affordable provision, in familiar settings, in the company of friends and neighbours and taught by inspiring teachers. 'Having a good time', 'making friends', 'feeling better about yourself', 'learning something useful or interesting' are all the sort of outcomes that make people come back for more.* (Thompson, 2004, p. 4)

It is paradoxical, therefore, that although the government claims to want to increase participation in learning, popular courses which act as a gateway to learning for many adults are being forced to close.

The narrowing of the curriculum coupled with higher fees could also have the effect of squeezing out groups of adults who have been habitually excluded in the past. At the same time, current planning and funding proposals could sharpen the class divide in the kinds of learning engaged in by adults. There is a danger that some providers will aim self-development provision at habitual learners who can afford to pay for it, a move that would result in this kind of learning becoming even more of a middle-class preserve. Although those on lowest incomes will be protected, there will be others for whom the increased costs of learning may be prohibitive:

> *We'll find that we end up with a service where if you've got enough money you can do anything from pottery to greyhound racing, but if you're not very well off you'll end up with just literacy, language and numeracy, ICT and parenting classes.* (Keep, quoted in Kingston, 2004a)

Cara (1999) wonders why it is assumed that poorer people want or need learning in areas such as parenting and LLN, rather than enrichment or self-development learning. She concludes that this assumption is the cultural legacy of an earlier policy environment:

> *It seems to me that the field has developed a particular hegemony over the past ten*

years, which may result from the split in the 1992 Act or may predate it, but which is certainly fed by the numerous regeneration funding opportunities which emphasise first step opportunities into vocational provision as appropriate for funding. The culture is so strong that given certain key prompts, and short term funding and the target group headings provide these, a certain curriculum offer is automatically generated. Given other prompts – a paying public, long-term mainstream funding – another curriculum, also quite predictable, emerges. These exist alongside each other, the first for those who won't join in and the second for the converted. (p. 20)

The loss of the diversity of learning programmes at the return-to-learn stage could result in an own goal for government by reducing possible routes to Level 2. This suggests that the lessons from some of the government's own commissioned investigations during the early 2000s may already have been forgotten. The government's Policy Action Teams' research on ways of encouraging social cohesion and neighbourhood renewal identified the loss of 'first rung' non-accredited provision as a consequence of the 1992 Further and Higher Education Act as one of the greatest obstacles to widening participation in the 1990s. This could well happen again.

Neglect of adults' aspirations and preferences

Policy aims and learner aims do not always coincide. While policy stresses raising skill levels and getting people into work, adults' purposes for learning are considerably wider and more diverse. Yet recent policy documents concentrate almost exclusively on the needs of employers and the labour market. But do only employer and business needs matter? It is odd that a government so obsessed with market demand in other policy areas ignores it in the area of adult education. This leads to the neglect of many adults whose purposes in learning do not include qualifications or employment. Moreover, if individual employability is such a priority, why is there so little emphasis on learning that contributes to this end?

In such a climate it is unsurprising that publicity for a recent national conference aimed at adult educators, entitled 'Skills for Employability', referred within the space of a few short paragraphs to: 'producing a workforce with the skills needed to meet the needs of business'; 'meeting the needs of business'; 'meeting the skills needs of employers'; 'producing employees with the skills that employers need'; and 'producing a workforce with the skills that meet the needs of business.' Taking its cue perhaps from the thrust of current policy, there is no mention in the publicity literature of employees' needs or helping individuals to develop the aptitudes, skills and knowledge they may require for their own current or future employment.

The neglect of learners' preferences contradicts the advice of national education agencies. Curriculum guidance from the QCA (2002) suggests that planning the post-16 curriculum should start with learners' own wishes rather than others' assumptions about what is best for them. It recommends that learners be enabled to contribute to shaping the curriculum according to their aspirations, strengths and interests, and to make their own choices about the activities and learning opportunities they join.

Similarly, Smith (2004) warns:

> *If we continue to 'decide what's best for learners' we will continue to miss those opportunities to develop self-esteem, skills of assertiveness and problem-solving which enable increasing learner autonomy and independence in the community.* (pp. 30–1)

Much of the advice relating to work with adults with learning difficulties could be applied to all adult learners. It is unfortunate, however, that the value attached in policy to external accreditation and tangible outcomes has been found to skew individual choices and aspirations, leading some individuals to participate in learning and assessment programmes that are inappropriate for them. Maudslay and Nightingale (2004), for example, refer to instances where adults with learning difficulties:

> *often wanted official accreditation even when this was not necessarily the best way of fulfilling their own aspirations. Similarly, some learners with learning difficulties will state their desire 'to learn reading and writing' because of its perceived status, whereas a focus on other wider skills might lead more appropriately to fulfilment of their overall aim.* (p. 32)

Maudslay and Nightingale (2004) call for more status to be attached to areas of learning that are not formally accredited. This echoes a sentiment that is widely expressed across the whole field of adult education:

> *It is time to look more fully and favourably upon the non-accredited forms of education. They are the starting gate for many, the pathways of individual educational progress, the open routes from which levels of qualification are achieved later. We squander our heritage if we fail to take seriously informal, non-accredited and social learning, and provide fully for it within our system.* (Gilbert, 2004, p. 21)

This is not to pretend that all is perfect with the traditional non-accredited adult curriculum. While there has been a 'clear and sustained improvement in the quality of adult and community learning', the ALI has identified weaknesses in curriculum planning, analysis of needs and attention to equal access (ALI, 2004). While some areas of the curriculum have been singled out for praise (art and design, health and care, family learning, ESOL and work with immigrants and asylum-seekers), other areas (language teaching, foundation programmes, and sports and leisure courses) have been judged unsatisfactory.

One of the challenges the Chief Inspector identifies for providers is to recognise the important role ACL can play in the context of the Skills Strategy and the social inclusion agenda, by offering high quality courses 'that meet the needs of individual learners, groups of learners, employers and communities alike' (ALI, 2004). (It is to be noted that learners are put first here rather than employers, which makes a refreshing change.) However, education providers will in future be faced with difficult decisions if they are to maintain a varied programme offer that meets so many different demands.

What is the purpose of adult learning?

Any discussion of the curriculum needs to consider what is the overall purpose of engaging in learning. As Mayo and Collymore (2000) ask, is it:

> *to transmit and reinforce existing norms and values or to promote critical reflection leading to challenges and social change – or both? Is the prime objective the attainment of 'useful knowledge' – instrumental skills and training – or really useful knowledge – which enables people to makes sense of the hardships and oppression they experience in their daily lives, and to develop strategies for greater equality and social justice. Is the focus primarily economic or is the focus wide enough to include social, cultural and political aims and objectives? Is there the space for education for active citizenship, and is there room for the learning needs of those who are not actively seeking paid employment. […] people with major caring responsibilities or people recovering from mental illness? And is the emphasis upon individual advancement alone or is there also room for group support and collective benefits for the local community?* (p. 142)

This thoughtful series of questions sets the wider, more inclusive aims of learning against the narrow and utilitarian one that is becoming the norm.

What is perhaps misunderstood, or not sufficiently recognised, is that learning that may not have explicit instrumental aims can lead to many of the outcomes that meet national priorities. There is evidence that good quality learning, whatever its focus, can assist in meeting goals such as improving citizenship and employment. The research conducted at the Centre for Research on the Wider Benefits of Learning, for example, has shown that attending 'leisure' courses in adult life has positive effects on health, social attitudes and civic and political participation.

Learning is valuable in its own right, not just as contribution to targets. However, it is not the targets per se that create a problem. Attempts to improve skills and levels of literacy and numeracy in England are wholly laudable. It is the exclusive focus on them at the expense of a broad and flexible curriculum that is creating an imbalance. But we need a broad and comprehensive curriculum if lifelong learning is ever to become a reality: one which includes, as well as LLN and skills for the labour market, education for active citizenship and education that enhances the quality of life

(Coffield, 2000). Unfortunately, we are facing the real possibility that these dimensions of the curriculum may continue to shrink. To quote a recent NIACE manifesto, to 'put the life back into adult learning' we need:

- *Rich and varied learning opportunities for everyone – irrespective of their age or employment status – to build a society of curious, creative, critical and confident people.*
- *A focus on learning that enables people to question and challenge in informed ways: learning that is connected to social and civic action and which transfers power from the powerful to the powerless.*
- *A focus on learning that respects people's differences and raises awareness about social justice, to help make our world a more equal and inspiring place to live in.*
- *Equal status for accredited and non-accredited learning.*
- *Funding for adult education that isn't dominated by crude labour market targets, that recognises the value of learning for personal fulfilment, social development and participatory democracy.*
- *Recognition that education is a right for all, not a privilege. Citizens should choose to learn and not be forced to join courses as a condition of benefit, work or citizenship.* (NIACE, 2005b)

If we want a fair and accessible system of adult education and if we want to widen participation in learning and encourage a lifelong learning culture, we have to keep a range of learning options open for adults. Sadly, as happened in the early 1990s, despite the commitment to protect wider learning opportunities, the broader aims and values of adult learning are being subordinated to narrow utilitarian purposes, and there is a real danger that innovation, creativity and inclusiveness in the curriculum may be sacrificed in the process.

References

Adult Learning Inspectorate (ALI) (2004) *Report on the Impact of Adult and Community Learning*. Coventry: ALI.

Aldridge, F. and Lavender, P. (1999) *The Impact of Learning on Health*. Leicester: NIACE.

All-Party Parliamentary Group for Further Education and Lifelong Learning (2004) *Insider Track: Prisoner Education in 2004 and Beyond*. The report of the All-Party Parliamentary Group for Further Education and Lifelong Learning's Inquiry.

Anderson, V. *et al.* (2005) *Count Me in FE: Research with LLDS and Their Experiences of Being Included Within Further Education*. London: Learning and Skills Development Agency.

Bhamra, K. (2004) T*he Wider Benefits of Non-Accredited Learning: Report of Research Findings*. London: West Learning Partnership.

Blunkett, D. (2000) *Learning and Skills Council Remit Letter*. Sheffield: Department for Education and Employment.

Bowman, H., Burden, T. and Konrad, J. (2000) *Successful Futures? Community Views of Adult Education and Training*. York: Joseph Rowntree Foundation.

Braggins, J. (2001) *Shared Responsibilities: Education for Prisoners at a Time of Change. Perceptions of Arrangements for the Delivery of Education for Prisoners in England and Wales in 2001*. NATFHE/Association of Colleges.

Cara, S. (1999) 'Is what's right for the rich not right for the poor?', *Adults Learning* 10(5), pp. 20–1.

Casey, H. (2005) 'Opinion', *Education Guardian Weekly*, 15 March, p. 15.

Cavanagh, D. (2000) 'Researching "inclusion": Reality and rhetoric; it's all in the curriculum approach'. In: A. Jackson and D. Jones (eds) *Papers from 30th annual conference of the Standing Conference on University Teaching and Research in the Education of Adults (SCUTREA)*, 3–5 July, University of Nottingham, pp. 35–40.

Chisholm, C., Haggart, J. and Horne, J. (2003) *Starting Points in Developing Wider Family Learning*. Leicester: NIACE.

Chisholm, L., Larson, A. and Mossoux, A-F. (2004) *Lifelong Learning: Citizens' Views in Close-Up*. Luxembourg: Office for Official Publications of the European Communities.

Coare, P. and Johnston, R. (2003) 'Section II: Community Voices,' in: P. Coare and R. Johnston (eds) *Adult Learning, Citizenship and Community Voices*. Leicester: NIACE.

Coffield, F. (2000) 'The structure below the surface: Reassessing the significance of informal learning'. In: F. Coffield (ed.) *The Learning Society: The Necessity of Informal Learning*. Bristol: The Policy Press, pp. 1–31.

Commission of the European Communities (2004) *Preparing a Collection of Key Statistics on Non-Vocational Adult Education in Europe*, Note from the commission, prepared for Grundtvig Working Group Meeting, 22/23 November 2004.

Cramb, M. (2004) *Progression on Non-Accredited Adult and Community Learning in London West*. Paper for LSC London West.

Department for Education and Employment (DfEE) (1998) *The Learning Age: A Renaissance for a New Britain*. London: The Stationery Office.

Department for Education and Employment (DfEE) (2000a) *Skills for Life: The National Strategy for Improving Adult Literacy and Numeracy Skills*. Sheffield: DfEE.

Department for Education and Employment (DfEE) (2000b) *Supporting Adult Learners: Guidance to Learning Partnerships*. Sheffield: DfEE.

Department for Education and Skills (DfES) (2002) *Adult Pre-Entry Framework for Literacy and Numeracy*. Sheffield: DfES.

Department for Education and Skills (DfES) (2003) *21st Century Skills: Realising our Potential*. Sheffield: DfES.

Department for Education and Skills (DfES) (2004) *Access to Learning for All*, Five-Year Strategy White Paper. Sheffield: DfES.

Department for Education and Skills (DfES) (2005) *Skills: Getting On in Business, Getting On at Work*, White Paper. Sheffield: DfES.

Department of Health (2000) *Valuing People: A New Strategy for Learning Disability in the 21st Century*. London: The Stationery Office.

Dimmock, C. and Foster, P. (2004) *Evaluation of the New Models of Move On and Get On at Work*. Research First Services.

Eldred, J. (2005) *Developing Embedded Literacy, Language and Numeracy: Supporting Achievement*. Leicester: NIACE.

Eldred, J., Ward, J., Snowdon, K. and Dutton, Y. (2005) *Catching Confidence: The Nature and Role of Confidence – Ways of Developing and Recording Changes in the Learning Context*. Leicester: NIACE.

Felstead, A., Gallie, D. and Green, F. (2002) *Work Skills in Britain 1986–2001*. Nottingham: DfES Publications.

Felstead, A. *et al.* (2005) *Better Learning, Better Performance: Evidence from the 2004 Learning At Work Survey*. Leicester: NIACE.

Flint, C. (2005) 'In defence of adult learning', *Adults Learning*, 16(6), p. 25.

Fullick, L. (2004) *Adult Learners in a Brave New World: Lifelong Learning Policy and Structural Changes Since 1997*. Leicester: NIACE.

Furedi, F. (2004) 'It's no longer critical and nor is it thinking', *Times Higher*, 24 September.

Further Education Funding Council (FEFC) (1996) *Inclusive Learning*. The report of the FEFC's Learning Difficulties and/or Disabilities Committee, chaired by Professor John Tomlinson. Coventry: FEFC.

Gilbert, H. (2004) 'Let a hundred flowers bloom', *Adults Learning*, 16(2), pp. 20–1.

Hillage, J., Uden, T., Aldridge, F. and Eccles, J. (2000) *Adult Learning in England: A Review*. NIACE/Institute for Employment Studies.

Horne, J. (2004) 'Building bridges', *Adult Learning & Skills*, Family Learning Edition, Issue 4, pp. 20–2.

Horne, J. and Haggart, J. (2004) *The Impact of Adults' Participation in Family Learning: A Study Based in Lancashire*. Leicester: NIACE.

James, K. (2001a) *Prescribing Learning: A Guide to Good Practice in Learning and Health*. Leicester: NIACE.

James, K. (2001b) *Prescriptions for Learning: Evaluation Report.* Leicester: NIACE.

James, K. (2004) *Winning Hearts and Minds: How to Promote Health and Well-Being through Participation in Adult Learning.* Leicester: NIACE.

James, K. and Nightingale, C. (2004) *Discovering Potential.* Leicester: NIACE.

Janssen, O. (2004) 'The impact of learning', *Adults Learning*, 15(9), pp. 24–6.

Kennedy, H. (QC) (1997) *Learning Works: Widening Participation in Further Education.* Coventry: FEFC.

Kent, N. (2004) 'Non-vocational education', Education Parliamentary Monitor, *Educational Journal*, issue 78.

Kingston, P. (2004a) 'Crisis, what crisis?', *Education Guardian Weekly*, 13 April.

Kingston, P. (2004b) 'Actions speak louder than words', *Education Guardian Weekly*, 9 November.

Kingston, P. (2005) 'WI backs college lobby', *Education Guardian Weekly*, 15 March.

Lamb, P. (2004) 'Challenges facing family learning', *Adult Learning & Skills*, Family Learning Edition, issue 4, pp. 13–4.

Lavender, P. (2004) 'Tests, targets and ptarmigans'. In: P. Lavender, J. Derrick and B. Brooks, *Testing, Testing... 1,2,3: Assessment in Adult Literacy, Language and Numeracy. A NIACE Policy Discussion Paper.* Leicester: NIACE, pp. 3–14.

Learning and Skills Council (LSC) (2004a) *Investing in Skills: Taking Forward the Skills Strategy.* An LSC Consultation Paper on Reforming the Funding and Planning Arrangements for First Steps, Personal and Community Development Learning for Adults. Coventry: LSC.

Learning and Skills Council (LSC) (2004b) *2002–03 National Learner Satisfaction Survey: Summary Report.* Coventry: LSC.

Learning and Skills Council (LSC) (2004c) *The Skills We Need: Our Annual Statement of Priorities.* Coventry: LSC.

Learning and Skills Research Centre (LSRC) (2004) *Emerging Policy for Vocational Learning in England: Will It Lead to a Better System?* London: LSRC.

Lewis, I. (2004) 'Getting the balance right?' Interview with Ivan Lewis, *Adults Learning*, 15(10), pp. 12–3.

Lochrie, M. (2005) 'Building all our futures', *Adults Learning*, 16(6), pp. 8–10.

London Skills Commission (2004) *Skilling for Inclusion: Enabling the Excluded to Access Learning and Sustainable Employment – Three Studies.* London Skills Commission.

Maudslay, L. and Nightingale, C. (2004) *Achievement in Non-Accredited Learning for Adults with Learning Difficulties.* Leicester: NIACE.

Mayo, M. and Collymore, A. (2000) 'Widening participation through Action Learning in the community'. In: J. Thompson (ed.) *Stretching the Academy.* Leicester: NIACE, pp. 141–57.

McGivney, V. (1994) *Summary Report 1: Economic Development Outcomes.* Gloucestershire LEA.

McGivney, V. (1995) 'Skills, knowledge and economic outcomes: A pilot study of adult learners in Gloucestershire', *Adults Learning*, 6(6), pp. 172–5.

McGivney, V. (2001) *Informal Learning in the Community.* Leicester: NIACE.

McGivney, V. (2003) *A Question of Value: Achievement and Progression in Adult Learning.* Leicester: NIACE.

Merton, A. and Greenwood, M. (2001) *You Mean It's OK to Ask... Evaluation of Non-Schedule 2 Projects 2000/2001.* NIACE/LSDA.

Morrell, J., Chowdury, R. and Savage, B. (2004) *Progression from Adult and Community Learning*, Research Report RR546, NOP Social and Political. Department for Education and Skills.

Moser, Sir C. (1999) *A Fresh Start: Improving Literacy and Numeracy*, Report of the Working Group, Department for Education and Employment. Sheffield: DfEE.

National Foundation for Educational Research (NFER) (2004) *Annual Survey of Trends in Education*, Digest no 16. NFER: Slough.

NIACE (2003a) *Embedding Literacy, Language and Numeracy. Final Report.* Unpublished. Leicester: NIACE.

NIACE (2003b) *Broad, Balanced and Embedded: Challenges and Starting Points in Developing Wider Family Learning Provision*, conference report. Leicester: NIACE.

NIACE (2003c) *NIACE Evaluation of LSC-Funded Family Learning Programmes: Final report.* Leicester: NIACE.

NIACE (2004) *Final Response from NIACE to the LSC Consultation Paper on Reforming the Funding and Planning Arrangements for First Steps and Personal and Community Development Learning for Adults*. Leicester: NIACE.

NIACE (2005a) *Parliamentary Questions Update: Summary of Response to Parliamentary Questions*, 23 March 2005. Leicester: NIACE.

NIACE (2005b) *Let's Put the Life Back into Adult Learning*. Leicester: NIACE.

NIACE and Foreign and Commonwealth Office (2003) *Bringing Education to Life: Reaching Hard-To-Reach Learners by Creating Innovative Approaches to Adult and Community Learning. A UK–Sweden initiative*. Foreign and Commonwealth Office and NIACE.

Office for Standards in Education (OFSTED) (2000) *Family Learning: A Survey of Current Practice*. London: HMSO.

Plimmer, G. (2004) 'Professional development: Back to the workshop management training', *Financial Times Report*, 11 October, p. 3.

Policy Action Team 10 (PAT 10) (1999) *A Report to the Social Exclusion Unit*. London: DCMS.

Preston, K. (2004) 'Lifelong learning & civic participation'. In: T. Schuller *et al.* (2004) *The Benefits of Learning*. London: RoutledgeFalmer.

Price, L. (2001) 'Pre-election perspectives', *Adults Learning*, 12(7), p. 12.

Qualifications and Curriculum Authority (QCA) (2002) *Designing a Learner-Centred Curriculum for 16–24 Year Olds with Learning Difficulties*. London: QCA.

Sargant, N. (2000) *The Learning Divide Revisited*. Leicester: NIACE.

Savitsky, F. (2004) 'My life has changed as a result of family learning', *Adult Learning and Skills*, Family Learning Edition, issue 4, pp. 11–12.

Schuller, T. *et al.* (2004) *The Benefits of Learning*. London: RoutledgeFalmer.

Sherlock, D. (2005) 'We must find ways of evaluating all learning – accredited or not', *Adults Learning*, 16(6), p. 19.

Smith, P. (2004) 'Learning to take control', *Adults Learning*, 16(2), pp 30–1.

Swain, J. (2004) 'Money isn't everything', *The Guardian*, 8 June.

Thompson, J. (2004) *Adult Learning and Community Renewal,* unpublished paper for the Counter Policy group.

Tuckett, A. (2001) *If I Can't Dance: Conviviality and Adult Learning.* Lecture given at University of East London, 24 January.

Tuckett, A. (2004) *Is Another World Possible?* Keynote speech given at conference 'Internationalization of lifelong education: policy and issues', Hong Kong, 4 December.

Tuckett, A. (2005) 'Robbing Peter to train Paul is no solution', *Times Education Supplement,* FE Focus section, 7 January, p. 4.

Turner, C. with Tuckett, A. (2003) *Catching the Tide: Areas of Consensus and Debate in the Recognition and Recording of Achievement in Non-Certificated Learning. A Policy Discussion Paper.* Leicester: NIACE.

Tyers, C. and Aston, J. (2002) *What Difference Did it Make? Impact of the Adult and Community Learning Fund.* Institute for Employment Studies (IES).

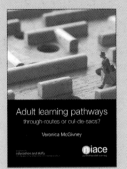

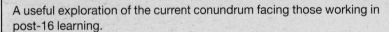